SACRED GEOGRAPHY

SACRED GEOGRAPHY

GEOMANCY: CO-CREATING THE EARTH COSMOS

MARKO POGAČNIK

LINDISFARNE BOOKS

2007

LINDISFARNE BOOKS
610 Main Street, Great Barrington, MA 01230
www.lindisfarne.org

LIBRARY OF CONGRESS CATALOGING-IN-PUBLICATION DATA

Pogacnik, Marko, 1944-
    Sacred geography : geomancy : co-creating the earth cosmos / Marko
Pogacnik.
        p. cm.
    ISBN 978-1-58420-054-3
    1. Geomancy. I. Title.
    BF1779.A88P64 2007
    133.3'33--dc22
                        2007025984

Contents

PART III
EARTH COSMOS — GEOMANTIC PHENOMENA

PART IV
GEOMANTIC PERCEPTION AND EXPLORATION

PART V
CREATING THROUGH GEOMANTIC KNOWLEDGE

CONCLUSION

PREFACE

This is my second effort to present geomancy as a whole to the public consciousness. I wrote my first book on this subject in German more than ten years ago, titled *School of Geomancy* (*Schule der Geomantie*, Knaur, Munich, 1996). However, since that time my knowledge of geomancy, coupled with my practical field work, has evolved and deepened to the extent that I was compelled to write a completely new book.

"Geomancy" is an ancient word denoting the knowledge of the invisible and the visible dimensions of the Earth and its landscapes. I see it as an essential complement to modern geography, which is exclusively interested in one level of reality only, the material level of existence. To convey the idea that geomantic knowledge in a very specific way complements the material point of view of geography, I refer to geomancy as "sacred geography." By "sacred" I mean that the task of geomancy in our present day is not simply to foster public interest in etheric, emotional and spiritual levels of places and landscapes, but also to promote a deeper, more loving, and more responsible relationship toward the Earth, the cosmos, and toward all beings, visible and invisible.

This book is conceived not only as a theoretical introduction to the worlds of sacred geography, but primarily as a practical guide through different dimensions of places and landscapes. It includes more than 170 practical examples from different parts of the world, all of them presented with original drawings. Much of the text, drawings and exercises are intended to describe and explain methods of pluridimensional perception, so that the reader will feel encouraged and supported to explore and develop her or his own experiences of the geomantic phenomena presented in the book.

My thanks go to my daughters Ana and Ajra Pogačnik, who provided essential help to me in the early 1990s to create the foundations of a holistic geomancy. My thanks go to Gene Gollogly, who years ago decided to present me and my work concerning the health of the Earth to the American public, and who has the courage to publish such a comprehensive volume. My third "thank you" goes to my longtime friend Leslie Luchonok, who volunteered to edit *Sacred Geography*.

Šempas, March 21, 2007
Marko Pogačnik

PART I

WELCOME BACK TO THE EARTH!

1.1 A holistic approach to natural sciences

FOR TOO LONG as a civilization we have been following the instructions of modern natural sciences concerning the identity of the Earth and its landscapes. The results of a strict rational perception of the planet's life can now be seen all around the globe in the form of innumerable degraded environments and an alienated consciousness of the Earth's inhabitants. The moment has arrived to recognize that the classical natural sciences are insufficient to deal properly with the heritage of the Blue Planet. The moment is ripe to search for another, more holistic approach to the Earth's identity and to its breath of life. Once found and formulated, this holistic venue can become a solid basis for developing a different, more loving and cooperative approach to the living planet and its evolutions.

One can see the ecological movement surging up within the last three decades as a kind of alternative to the classical natural sciences. Unfortunately, as a daughter of classical natural sciences, ecology refers to the same rational paradigm that does not allow the Earth to be loved while being explored and protected. As a result, ecological endeavors stay on the surface of life's web, ignoring the subtle dimension of Earth, its beings and environments.

The holistic approach means not only to acknowledge all levels of existence, the so-called visible and invisible, but also to foster a human presence within the web of life. The moment has come to open to the multidimensionality of the Earth and its evolutions. The moment has come to renounce the highly prized distance between the human being as a subject and the Earth as the object of interest and research. Or, more precisely, within the holistic paradigm, the subject-object approach is only one of the possible entries to the organism of the Earth. Knowledge equally rich can be obtained through loving the Earth and perceiving it through the means of one's intuition.

1.2 Geomancy as an alternative to the language of geography

If we speak of a need to develop a holistic approach to the Earth, its vital-energy network, its consciousness and its sacred dimensions, we do not intend to revive one of the geomantic systems related to ancient cultures and past epochs. The Earth is an organism of constant change, and is even more rapidly affected by cycles of transformation in human consciousness.

The effort invested into the present book project, and the related practice, aims at formulating a basic knowledge upon which an updated relationship to the planetary organism/consciousness can be developed. This new holistic relationship can further serve as an inspiration toward a more harmonious way of cooperation between human culture and the Earth, locally and globally.

It may sound a bit contradictory, but the holistic language presented through this book project is called "geomancy"—contradictory in the sense that we are aiming at a modern approach to nature and the Earth Cosmos, and yet we are using an ancient term. "Geomancy" is composed of two Greek words—one standing for the Earth (Gea or Gaia)—and the other one for divination (Gr. "mantein")—Geomancy!

The decision to use the term "geomancy" refers to the modern use of the name Gaia for the living and conscious Earth. The term "divination" might properly express our interest for the sacred and invisible dimensions of the Earth as complementary to those visible and material extensions described through the language of geography.

Blending ecology and shamanic tradition

What are the decisive steps we can take to develop and support this new holistic approach, allowing geomancy to rise to public awareness and propose relevant solutions to our current planetary crisis? First of all, forget about any geomancy teaching of the past! The geomancy we are considering here rises out of the creative imagination of many individuals who love the Earth and its multifaceted cosmos, who are willing to listen to its message without being attached to any tradition.

Second, forget about any conceptual predispositions! Experience is what secures a solid foundation for geomantic knowledge to be developed and made practical. We must learn to listen to the multi-dimensional reality of the Earth. Heart-to-heart experience is needed as a basis upon which scientific patterns of understanding can then be formulated.

Third, ecology has inspired us to undertake practical steps in protecting life upon the Earth. However, in order for our efforts to become more successful, we need to integrate our common shamanic heritage that all cultures worldwide share. What do we mean by the shamanic heritage? Talk to the Earth, to the animals, plants, and nature spirits! Be present within the whole of which you are a holographic part. Talk to the stars, to our ancestors who are our predecessors. Celebrate the beauty and systematic order of the visible world, yet also gather the knowledge of the Earth Cosmos to which the eye of our mind might be blind. Find the points of synergy. Combine inner experiences with the capability of the rational mind to make geomantic knowledge work practically in our epoch of crisis and transformation.

Let us put aside our preconceptions. It is life that matters!

1.3 The concept of multidimensional reality

To be able to proceed toward a more holistic perception of the Earth, landscape, and nature we need to question the modern concept of space and time as an exclusive framework within which our reality evolves. In effect, if one looks upon the way different cultures worldwide function, an alternative to the materialistic space and time concept already exists. We know that within each culture there are believers in sacred dimensions of life that our rational mind cannot encompass.

Human beings are obviously capable of imagining a "nonrational" plane of existence that is all-embracing, that precedes any form or concept. The best way to call this plane of existence might be the *dimension of eternity*. One can imagine that the spiritual essence of the human being, the so-called *inner self*, takes part in that same *ocean of infinity*.

On the other hand, humans generally take part in a global civilization that is strictly profane. This civilization functions almost exclusively on a rational level according to the framework of linear time and so-called three-dimensional space, as do our computers. We sit firmly within our material bodies and perceive reality as a multitude of more or less physical forms. At this level human beings relate to their watches and to the linear time that passes second by second. We can speak of the *material dimension of reality*, its exclusive *space-and-time dimension*.

An *ocean of infinity* versus a *material dimension of reality*: neither of these two modes of existence can be denied. Yet there are three major problems hidden in such a classical opposition between spirit and matter.

First, modern human beings have lost the ability to experience themselves as taking part in the vast ocean of eternity while simultaneously walking in a physical body through relatively narrow space and time structures. This causes a dangerous schism within the modern human psyche.

Secondly, the modern human being has lost the sense of other beings, like mountains, trees, elephants, and stars, taking part in the same ocean of infinity as we do. As a global civilization we have become extremely anthropocentric. The common basis that all beings and manifestations of life or non-life share is lost to our consciousness.

There is a third problem to solve. The pulsation of eternity cannot properly imbue matter with the breath of life if there are no intermediate dimensions that allow communication between the two extremes. The condition in which the two extremes are separated—the ocean of eternal vibration and the material structures of the body—we call death. Do we aim for death?

To introduce some intermediate steps between the abstract presence of eternity and the bodily structures of space and time, we have to become conscious of three other dimensions of reality that permeate human beings, landscapes, nature worlds, and the Earth as a whole. I mean the *soul dimension*, the *dimension of consciousness*, and the so-called *etheric dimension*.

Let us list the proposed five dimensions of an all-encompassing reality. We apologize for listing them in a hierarchical way, due to the linear body of the classical book structure. The accompanying drawing (on page 7) may be a more relevant visual representation.

1. The broadest and the most unlimited dimension of reality that we can think of—or experience—is the *dimension of eternity*. As mentioned above, we can also use the expression *ocean of infinity*. We can address this dimension of reality as primeval vibration, the divine all-presence, the light of light. Within a given landscape *the dimension of eternity* can be experienced practically as a most sacred level of reality, manifested perhaps as a landscape temple or a sacred site.

2. Next follows the *soul dimension*, which can also be called the *archetypal dimension* of reality. Out of the ocean of infinity arise qualities that have a clear sense of purpose and identity, but no forms, not even forms that we could compare with our thoughts or emotions. Each manifested form refers to a certain archetype or archetypal being (a soul) pulsating within the archetypal dimension of reality. Practically this dimension manifests on the Earth's surface as the voice of Gea, the soul of planetary creation, as angelic presence or archetypal patterns behind reality.

3. The third dimension of this multidimensional reality may be called the *dimension of consciousness*. On this level cosmic ideas, archetypes, and beings become operational. Communication begins on this level, as well as conscious reflection of what is going on and what may need to be done. The dimension of consciousness covers a great range of manifestations, from mental to emotional consciousness,

from intuitive to rational. Practically one encounters the consciousness dimension within a given landscape in the form of elemental
beings, nature's environmental spirits that embody the Gaia's consciousness. In addition, patterns of human behavior that one dis-
covers in the landscape are related to the consciousness dimension
of reality.

4. Approaching denser extensions of multidimensional reality, we
   arrive within the field of the *etheric dimension*. It might be more
   properly called the *vital-energy dimension* (or the *bio-energetic
   dimension*). There is no form yet, but an intense flow of life forces.
   This dimensions of reality does not concern physical forms of energy
   but etheric ones ("bios" stands in Greek for life, "vita" in Latin).
   We use the expression "life force" to refer to what the Hindus call
   "prana" or what the Chinese speak of as "chi." According to the
   Greek concept of the five elements, the element of ether represents
   the invisible element beyond the manifested four elements. In this
   sense the expression *etheric dimension* is particularly appropriate.
   Vital-energy fields, Earth chakras, and channels of vital power are
   all manifestation of the etheric dimension of the landscape.

5. At last we have arrived at the ground level. The fifth dimension
   could be called the *material dimension*. It is the dimension in which
   embodiment of minerals, plants, animals, human beings, landscape
   features, stars and the Earth's crust takes place. We know it as the
   physical world, or as the world of form. What existed before in the
   landscape as something invisible now takes on material form and
   becomes perceptible by the outer senses. It finds its manifestation
   within the structures of linear time and physical space.

Please remember—one should not see the five dimensions of reality as ruled by a hierarchical pattern. They all exist at the same time,
vibrating simultaneously at different frequencies and representing different qualities of density.

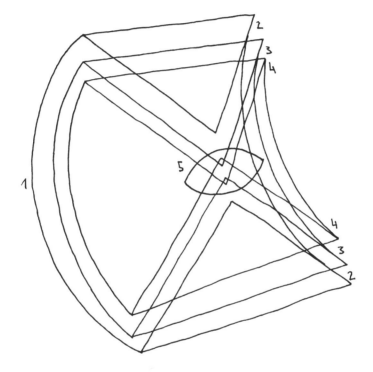

Scheme representing the five-dimensional space concept—the numbers refer to the explanation above of the five dimensions.

1.4 It all depends on the mode of perception

As long as it is not possible to perceive and experience the five dimensions of multidimensional reality, the above scheme represents no more than a possible concept. In effect, human beings generally will not be capable of perceiving any dimension other than the materialized one. The five senses that we currently use enable us to move perfectly within the structures of linear time and physical space. Yet they are useless in perceiving the other four dimensions. Consequently we simply perceive other dimensions as nonexistent.

There is an obvious contradiction in this situation. Even if human beings embody all five dimensions of reality, we perceive and thus experience only one of them as real. This unnatural situation is a result of our over-enthusiastic interest in expanding the rational aspect of our consciousness over thousands of years. Since the rational mind now generally serves as the exclusive interpreter of our perceptions, we now perceive only the portion of reality that can be processed and understood by rational thought and logic. All other layers of information that we may perceive are blocked and stored in our subconscious. They are prevented from reaching the light of our awareness.

We do not need additional organs of perception to change the evolutionary course that has blinded us to larger portions of reality, but only a new mode of becoming aware of reality around us. The basic endeavor of a new geomancy is to develop the potentials within the human being to become conscious of all the different layers of reality that surround us and that simultaneously pulsate within ourselves. The primary task of modern geomancy is to explore, learn and teach alternative modes of perception.

We do not need to develop special abilities to perceive the so-called invisible dimensions of reality. The capacity of multidimensional perception does not depend on special gifts. It is a most democratic capacity that all people share. We simply need to change our mode of perception. The rational mind perceives reality by taking itself out of the whole, thus looking upon the world from outside. As a result of this subjective-objective split only the coarsest level, the material dimension of reality, can be seen.

The approach and technique used in geomancy is an opposite one. One learns to become one with the "object" of perception. By becoming one with the object it is possible to receive or cultivate an inner experience of its different dimensions and facets. Perception is not based on separation but rooted in oneness, in the intimate sharing of the sense of beingness between two subjects. Not separation, but a sense of love is needed to experience life in its multifaceted reality.

There are several tools at our disposal to approach this kind of inner experience. The sensitivity of our auric fields is one of them. An experience may touch our emotional fields and leave an imprint or impression that can later be interpreted. Some bodily reactions may occur that again can be understood later. The consciousness of the perceiver may react by producing some images, light figures, or symbols related to the essence of the experienced phenomena. Our intuition may serve as a device through which the perceived phenomena can reveal itself in its totality. However, becoming one with a certain aspect of life's web (or multidimensionality) and the following inner experiences of the given phenomena are only the first two steps in the process of holistic perception. These experiences can and should be followed by a third step in which the rational mind (perhaps coupled with our intuition) attempts to interpret the perceived information. The various aspects of holistic perception may be compared to each other to derive or understand a sense of the underlying truth. This experience can be formulated in a logical form so that it can be transmitted to others, or serve as the basis for a specific practical decision. In this way the multidimensional perception process can arrive upon solid ground!

It is crucial to understand that the deeper dimensions of reality can be perceived only under some basic ethical preconditions. If one is not connected to the divine essence within oneself and the world around, one cannot expect valuable perceptions to occur. If one is not at peace inside and well-grounded outside, one's inner perceptions will be disturbed and distorted. The dependence of holistic perception on these ethical qualities does not lessen its value. On the contrary, people must respect life within and around them to take part in its wholeness! Otherwise we remain blind to it. Changing our mode of perception means to choose a world of mutual respect, love, and cooperation. Adopting holistic perception also implies a political decision—meaning that the world can change into one of harmony and pan-democracy. Pan-democracy means that all beings visible and invisible share a common world space—which of course cannot be but pluridimensional.

1.5 Geomancy oscillating between art and science

Imagining a new planetary cosmos, a much more balanced and all-embracing space of reality, is in itself a creative act. All those who take part in the process of adopting and exploring the ideas and tools of holistic geomancy, who start to implement them within their thinking or to weave them into their daily practice, are at the same time working on further developing its essence. Space and time structures are not automatic—they need to be re-created in each moment in order to exist and to help different life forms evolve. The obvious aim of holistic geomancy is to change our ruling space and time concepts and alter the temporal and spatial reality of everyday life.

In this sense geomancy can be perceived as an artistic venture rather than a scientific discipline. Its primary impulse is to create a new and original point of view and to explore multifaceted reality on the basis of personal sensitivity, imagination, and intuition—all of which are characteristics of artistic work. In this sense geomancy is an artistic discipline. Its creative range and its tools are discussed in more detailed in Chapter 5.

We also mentioned that there cannot be reliable or accurate results of perception if the perceiver is not present, grounded and inwardly connected within his/her core self. We stressed the importance of the ethical foundation of geomantic work in relationship to the results obtained in the perception and exploration of multidimensional reality. Working on one's own ego-detachment and unconscious thought patterns and paying attention to one's personal alignment are preconditions for a human being to be free in creating the new Earth Cosmos.

At the same time that geomancy can be considered an artistic endeavor it can be also seen as incorporating characteristics of modern science. Geomancy tends to develop an exact language and a conscious, systematic approach to the Earth reality. It is conscious of its own paradigm. Even more, holistic geomancy is ready to take an active role in our collective responsibility for the state of the world. It is not an esoteric discipline rearranging its own world. Geomancy, as envisioned throughout this book and its related practice, is seeking to offer solutions to the problems of the world that we all share. Holistic geomantic approaches and concepts for a more harmonious co-existence of the natural world and human culture need to be heard and implemented here and now.

Modern natural sciences, including geography, are shaping the destiny of our civilization and our Earth planet. Through the perspective of a developing geomantic science it is possible to identify some of the major flaws of the rational sciences that have contributed to our present-day environmental crisis. The purpose of holistic geomancy is to propose and implement practical alternatives and solutions, and to ensure that holistic insights will be included when decisions are being made and implemented about how to relate to the different aspects and extensions of the Earth Cosmos.

1.6 Artistic creativity shaping our daily reality

Too often artistic creativity is taken as a cultural supplement and not as a decisive co-creator of our daily reality. The Renaissance masters of spatial perspective, like Ucello, Mantegna, or Leonardo da Vinci, changed the way modern human beings see the world around themselves. The perspective view that these masters invented taught us to perceive shapes of the materialized world in a much more three-dimensional and accurate way. As a result the rise of precise and objective scientific research became possible during the following centuries.

The modern art movement, starting in the nineteenth century with impressionism, abstract painting, and other streams like surrealism introduced the next revolutionary step in our perception. Our eyes were opened to alternative visions of reality. It became possible to visualize worlds and dimensions other than those created by the strict logic of the rationally structured world. The conceptual art of the 1960s, with its concepts, performances, and installations, went further. It stimulated reflection about one's own point of view and possibilities for changing our perspectives, this time on a spiritual level. Thus new ways of seeing and creating the space of reality have become possible through art.

The holistic, ecologically engaged approach to landscape and art inspired by the knowledge of geomancy represents the next step in the process. With a new phase starting in the mid-1980s, new ways of perceiving and understanding life and the space of reality become more practical. Artistic practice becomes a tool to enable human beings to interact with different extensions of daily reality. Artistic language makes it possible, for example, to work on decoding the essence of a specific landscape or to contribute to the healing of its ecological problems.

So here we are now, thinking, envisioning, and practicing alternative ways of approaching the Earth planet and its different landscapes and dimensions at the threshold of the twenty-first century. To a great extent the revolutionary path of thinking, feeling, and creating pioneered by many generations of artists has helped lead the way to our pilgrimage into the world of the sacred geography.

1.7 Why back to the Earth?

To understand the reason for our renewed interest in the Earth's different dimensions we first need to introduce the idea of space. Space should not be understood as something existing far out in the universe. Within the geomantic thought system the term "space" denotes a special order according to which the multifaceted reality of a certain life unit is organized. In this sense we may speak of the Earth space, the space of a valley, the space of one's heart or the universal space.

The current constitution of the Earth's space comes into being through a very limited cooperation between the rational mind on one side and the consciousness of nature, including its life forces, on the other. It is a result of a millennia-long process during which the collective human mind has selected only those elements of the multidimensional reality that can be addressed through rational thought and causal logic. We currently perceive and live in space as a rationally structured extract of reality, not reality itself.

During the last two centuries our civilization has spread upon the Earth by extensively using the resources of the planet without relating to the foundations and multidimensional reality of life described above. As a result, we are now facing harmful ecological trends like global warming and the threat of a total destruction of life on the planet.

The invitation to come back to the Earth implies that the space in which we presently live represents an abstract mental structure, rather than a place where a holistic experience of the Earth's reality can be lived. *Coming back to the Earth* means detaching inwardly from the rationally structured Earth's space and opening one's consciousness and perception to the different dimensions of its true ecosphere. Come and get to know the planet anew!

A surprise: meanwhile, the Earth has changed!

Pay attention! Developing a holistic approach to the planet's multidimensionality in the context of the considerations described above implies initiating a major change within the governing space structure. The etheric foundations of a new, never before experienced Earth space can start to emerge. Surprisingly this is exactly what geomantic perceptions of the last decade reveal. At the end of the twentieth century basic changes within human consciousness toward a holistic world view have become so strong that Gea, the Earth Soul, has started to react. Since late 1997 it is possible to perceive drastic changes within the planetary space structure. Geomantic phenomena not known before occur. New generations of nature spirits appear, related to a surprisingly open type of consciousness. A strong wave toward transmuting and recycling destructive powers and rigid patterns has been set into motion.

Considering a more holistic approach to the Earth, its different worlds, and its dimensions can succeed in creating a new culture of peace between Gea and humanity. This new culture can be created with constant cooperation between the two major partners of the Earth's evolution. On one hand the Earth Soul is creating new spatial conditions, releasing a strong impulse toward changing the egoistic and rationally limited state of being of billions of people worldwide. The greater purpose is clear—to awaken these billions to the true essence of life, their deeper identity, and the true essence of our home planet. At the same time, human individuals and groups, entering upon the process of personal change and working consciously to transmute old limiting social, political, and economic patterns, enable the Earth Soul to develop a new planetary cosmos, a much more balanced and all-embracing space of reality, a true *Earth Cosmos*—our future planetary home.

PART II

LANDSCAPE, GEA-CONSCIOUSNESS, OTHERWORLD

2.1 Evolution beyond mere reasoning

Stretch your imagination!

BEFORE WE ARE ready to dedicate our attention to individual geomantic phenomena, we need to do some exercises in stretching our imagination so that we can encompass the incredible rich inventory of the pluridimensional world.

The intention of the second part of this book is not to provide final and complete concepts about evolution, consciousness, and different worlds. Our primary intention is to experiment with possibilities yet dormant within our human mind that once awakened, will enable us to become more open toward alternative paths of thinking, feeling and imagining.

Taking the concept of evolution as our first exercise ground, let's briefly remember the preceding chapter on the multidimensional space of reality. Given that universal space is pluridimensional, and given the interlacing of different strands of consciousness and development, it does not feel right to reduce our thinking to one stream of evolution, generally referred to as the materialistic (Darwinist) model of development.

What geologists have presented to our rational, reasoning mind is only that aspect of the evolutionary stream that over billions of years has found its expression within the material extension of the Earth's ecosphere. The hardening of the Earth core, the appearance of water and oceans, the coming and going of ice ages, and the evolution of plants, animals, and human beings are all phenomena that are related to evolution at the material level of existence.

It is true that the material level of the universe is so perfect in itself, so full of beauty and surprise, that no other dimension of existence seems to be needed to supplement its evolution. However, this approach leads us nowhere. According to the holographic principle with which we are going to experiment a bit later, each layer of reality is relatively autonomous and perfect in itself. At the same time the quality of its autonomy and perfection depends on all other dimensions of cosmic reality. Even if these dimensions are invisible, they are inseparable for the whole to exist as it is.

I believe that when the ancients considered the material world, and referred to it as maya, or "illusion," they did not mean that the material dimension of reality is illusionary in itself. They meant, however, that the source of illusion is the reasoning mind's preconception that the material world is capable of standing upright and functioning on its own, limited to its own sphere. Unfortunately, we presently abide within a global civilization that endeavors to put this limited concept of evolution into practice. We should not be astonished that the generally perceived reality around us is breaking down under the pressure of illusionary preconceptions.

Soul purpose

Are there other evolutionary streams that are providing the basis for the material dimension of reality to enfold its beauty?

Let's first clarify a basic premise. It is not possible to speak of any kind of evolutionary movement within the space of eternity. It is not possible to imagine eternity moving in a specific direction. *Evolutionary movement comes into being only at the level of the soul.*

Let us then speak about the *evolution of the Earth Soul*, consciously moving toward the materialization of its divine essence, giving form to its archetypal ideas. From this evolution we enjoy living landscapes, vibrating minerals, breathing plants, animals moving from place to place, and the beauty and thrill of creative inspiration.

It is difficult to believe that without the driving power of a soul purpose a planet would invest billions of years into the movement of physical matter toward a living and evolving environment, full of beauty and excitement. I believe that it is the driving power of Gea's soul purpose that evolutionary beings of the Earth experience as "love of Mother Earth." To be constantly bathed in that love on a practical level means to be led by Gea's soul purpose toward more and more perfected forms of incarnation within physical matter.

Another example of evolution at the soul level is the revolutionary attempt of two powerful soul beings of the universe, Buddha and Christ, who incarnated upon the Earth to teach humankind about a new kind of world order that does not depend on hierarchical relationships. They taught and demonstrated two models of behavior that could help human beings escape the control of mental (mind) systems and reach spiritual freedom. By stepping out of the predestined wheel of life, or through selfless service to all beings, it is possible (this is how their message may be translated into modern terms) to become *the co-creator of one's life and destiny*. By opening a totally new perspective upon life they, and other such powerful soul beings, have changed the course of evolution.

Today we have a multitude of individuals who are attuning to the cosmic whole and are capable of listening to the voice of their inner self. We should not underestimate the power of this movement on Gea's evolutionary course, and the corresponding hope and opportunity for positive change. Millions of people worldwide are creating constructive alternatives and putting them into action, following the inspiration of their inner soul essence.

No less important to the Earth's evolution are the contributions of our ancestors, human souls who presently are not incarnated within material bodies. Many of these ancestors are conscious of the needs of the planetary evolution. One can imagine them as brotherhoods/sisterhoods that focus on different matters within our evolution that need impulses of change or support. In their present state of being they cannot act on our material reality, but they are capable of telepathically inspiring us to act, or of guiding us along the paths of change and transformation.

Consciousness, vital energies, and form evolution

The traditional Trinitarian model, as formulated within many different planetary cultures, may be used in an approach to understanding the multi-layer concept of the Earth's evolution. The principle of "the Father" (Allah in Islamic tradition) stands for the ocean of eternity.

The principle of "the Son" (the Christ of Western culture) symbolizes the creative act, the soul purpose behind the evolutionary drive. The third principle, known in the Christian tradition as "the Holy Spirit," represents the powers of manifestation that allow the reality of existence and material forms to be experienced and perceived.

The first two principles have already been discussed above. The third principle gives rise to the evolution of civilizations that translate spirit into form. As an example, let us consider the evolution of elemental beings or environmental spirits. We have generally referred to these beings as "nature spirits." But we now live in a world that is progressively dominated by material forms and structures. We need to acknowledge that there must be a growing multitude of nature spirits that engage not only in nature, but also within this world of material forms and structures created by human beings. To cover both of these aspects of creation, let's call these spirits "environmental spirits."

The world of environmental spirits and elemental beings is crucial at that moment when the soul imaginations of Gea, the inner essence of the Earth, are clothed in form and become alive within different life streams. A special type of consciousness is needed to mediate between the ideas emanating from the heart of the Earth and the consequent manifested creation on the Earth.

Therefore the Earth Soul has given rise to an evolution of consciousness that is capable of listening to the archetypal language of the Earth Soul. Environmental spirits posses a kind of light body composed of vital ethers, in order to approach plants, minerals, animals, and human beings—those beings who live in the materialized world. Elemental and environmental beings guide these forms of creation on their evolutionary path through the material world. They know the archetypal blueprint of a particular evolution and its timetable of development, and how to move life energies and attract needed cosmic impulses.

The rise of civilizations

The way in which human beings evolve does not occur only along the path of nature's evolution, but also along the path of different civilizations that succeed each other, or that even run parallel to each other on various levels of reality. A human being is a kind of composite being. Part of us belongs to the evolution of the Earth. We eat, sleep, and perform sex as do other higher evolved members of the animal evolution. In this sense we take part in the evolution of the Earth's biosphere.

At the same time, as a vast group of individualized souls, we are children of eternity and belong to the evolution of cosmic consciousness, as do other evolutions such as angelic beings. In collaboration with the Earth Soul, cosmic consciousness created an intricate path of birth, death, and rebirth (the so-called path of reincarnation) to enable individual human souls to successively take part in cosmic consciousness and earthly space.

Moving rhythmically back and forth between these dimensions, we build different civilizations through which the cosmic and the earthly dimensions creatively relate to each other. All beings of the Earth and universe benefit from the resulting collaboration. As human beings we are presented with a fantastic variety of opportunities to ground our creative ideas, to manifest them in form. We feel enthusiastic about seeing our abstract concepts become a tangible reality. We have the opportunity to experience material reality within our own bodies, and to direct divine consciousness or the powers of the Earth Soul for selfish or destructive means, or for selfless and constructive purposes. How grateful we are for what we can learn in this way!

The Earth Soul and its evolutions may also be grateful for this collaboration with human civilizations, for the opportunity to experience their consciousness and destiny involved with all kinds of creative processes that human beings discover, invent, explore. For example, there are domesticated plants and animals that did not exist prior to the rise of civilizations. Consider also elements or minerals (like silica) whose essential qualities are used in processing ways of human thinking and memory within the circuits of a computer!

2.2 We cannot avoid some theological themes

Cosmic duality: Yin and Yang

As an approach to understanding the path of evolution, we described the Trinitarian archetype above. This archetype is based upon the linear (masculine) principle of succession from the first to the second, and from the second to the third. The path leads from the ocean of eternity (1) to the individualization of archetypal ideas/souls (2), and from there to manifestation in the form of consciousness, energy and form (3). But to be able to follow the specific time rhythm through which evolutionary streams manifest within the world of consciousness, energy, and form, we need to introduce the feminine principle, a principle based upon cyclic rhythms.

The traditional way to characterize the complementary principles of masculine and feminine, which are decisive for shaping universal reality, is to speak of solar and lunar poles. Using theological language, we speak of the God and Goddess presence. The Eastern world is more used to the expressions Yang and Yin. We could also speak of two poles of reality that correspond to the linear and cyclic principles.

It is possible to use the relative terms "positive" for the solar (Yang) and "negative" for the lunar (Yin) principle, with the condition that neither is considered "bad." Both principles play a creative role within the organism of the whole. When life is about to manifest in any form, the manifestation occurs through the interaction of the two opposing and complementing poles. We, humanity, are learning how to maintain harmony between the opposites—wisdom. Our aim is to be different, individual, and yet part of a joyful whole.

The cyclic principle: the threefold Goddess

One way to present the cyclic principle (Yin) as it works within nature, within a given landscape, or within the psychic world of a human being is through the image of the threefold Goddess. This image or archetype refers to experiences gathered by different cultures over millennia about how the Divine Feminine manifests within the flow of daily life and within seasonal and cosmic cycles. The Divine Feminine basically manifests through a succession of three phases that relate to the three phases of the moon—the new moon (with a symbolic color of white), the full moon (red), and the dark moon (black).

We can consider the image of the threefold Goddess as a specific language, a language which can be used to explain the working of the feminine principle within evolution, within the cycles of personal life, or within a portion of landscape. Let's briefly reconstruct the basics of that language, which can be very usefully applied to interpreting geomantic phenomena, especially those related to the sacred dimension of landscape. (For more complex insights refer to my book *The Daughter of Gaia*.)

1. The holistic aspect

The cycle starts with the phase of wholeness and all-connectedness. The holistic phase is symbolized by the Virgin Goddess and her ability to hold the whole diversity of the universe in oneness. Other symbols include the rising quality of the new moon and the color white. In the northern hemisphere the white phase of the Goddess is experienced as spring and in one's personal life as the phase of inspiration. Seeds begin to germinate, new ideas start to glow in one's consciousness. There is no action or reaction at this moment, no polarization, simply the basic quality of the White Goddess as pure presence.

2. The creative aspect

During the second phase of the threefold cycle the feminine-masculine polarity comes into being. Symbolic language refers to the Red Goddess phase, the phase of the sacred marriage between the opposites, the phase of the full moon. The phase of the Red Goddess represents the creative phase, the phase of adulthood, the phase of doing and manifesting. Within each human being, within each woman and man, the masculine (Yang) and feminine (Yin) aspects interact to enable growth, learning, and expanding consciousness.

3. The aspect of transmutation

Following the creative phase, a phase of crisis and decomposition becomes inevitable. Individuals and cultures experience the rise of destructive forces that undermine outmoded patterns of social, moral, or political behavior. In the language of the Goddess, we are entering the phase of death and resurrection, the phase of the Black Goddess. Her powers of transmutation create the setting for the transition from the old to a new cycle of birth and creativity.

In using the image of the threefold Goddess as a language to understand life processes we are going beyond logical, linear thinking. At the same time that the rational mind is thinking in a specific language, we are invited to dance with the underlying archetype, which is beyond language. While the human mind uses the image of the threefold Goddess to perceive the sacred dimension of a landscape, the Goddess, or the feminine essence of the universe, also uses this same rational capacity of our mind to confirm its immediate presence in material reality.

The role of evil and opposing forces

The Black Goddess archetype described above provides for a phase of crisis and decomposition that follows creativity, a cyclic process that ushers in the release and transformation of outmoded patterns of social, moral, or political behavior. It is important to understand this as a natural, beneficial, and inevitable process in much the same way as a gardener observes the change of seasons, and prepares compost to fertilize a future cycle of new growth and expansion. Death and destruction are commonplace and necessary parts of a larger cycle.

At the same time, Gea, the Earth Soul, may also usher in destructive forces in response to inappropriate or destructive actions initiated by humankind that are not in harmony with her vital energies, landscape, and ecosystems. Whatever we do within the Earth Cosmos, we are using the powers of the Earth Soul. Doesn't it make sense that Gea has negative powers at her disposal to respond or react to destructive actions in order to bring about a greater realignment of life on the planet?

The problem of the misuse of Earth energy can be further exacerbated when humans intentionally use Gea for purposes of power and greed, for control and exploitation. We can also manipulate natural powers and life process in ways that can result in life energies that are destructive and poisonous. For example, in its essence atomic power is an etheric power. If we use this power solely on a material level, as our civilization does (for electric power and weapons), we turn its life forces into powers of death, especially when we do not have the capacity to control what we have created. Genetic engineering presents a similar problem. The genetic code of living beings is an expression of the archetypal soul level. Manipulating the genetic code exclusively through rational consciousness and for material ends may cause unprecedented destruction and loss for life.

However, if the powers of the Earth Soul are abused in such a way that they become destructive, the powers of the Earth Soul can also be recycled and brought back to their natural cycle. (See Chapter 3.10.)

Love and wisdom embodied

We humans enjoy observing different landscapes, moving through their tapestry, and experiencing the colors and sensations of the different seasons. But when we consider our relationship to the divine we generally turn away from our earthly nature, as if the two were separate. Our human minds tend to identify our earthly nature and Gea's landscape within the narrow space and time of material embodiment, due simply to the fact that we do not recognize the spiritual and soul dimensions of the Earth. Within the human subconscious there is a pattern of alienation or hostility toward the essence of the Earth. We tend to believe that the Earth and nature are but a temporary home of the human soul, and that sooner or later we will die and depart from this temporary home.

However, spiritual teachers over millennia have identified our soul essence with the body of the Earth, conveying the message that we can experience the quality of the divine through and with the Earth. We can experience divinity here, not necessarily in the vast cosmos, and be in harmony with God within the Earth space, touching and feeling its Presence!

Unfortunately Western culture and religious institutions have missed much of the message conveyed by Jesus the Christ concerning his relationship to the Earth Cosmos. It was primarily through experiences, not words, that the planetary dimension and importance of this relationship was transmitted to his fellow human beings. Another misunderstanding of his teaching is related to the nature of time. As a (Western) culture we relate to his incarnation on Earth two millennia ago, instead of relating to the Christ as a cosmic archetype of love and wisdom, pulsating and radiating within each particle of the Earth Cosmos *now*. (For further insights see *How Wide the Heart*, a book that I co-wrote with my daughter Ana.)

So what is the problem in relating to the divine love and wisdom within the Earth? There is no problem, rather an opening to further understanding and evolution. In the vastness of eternity, the human soul is absorbed by divine love and wisdom. Yet within the Earth holon, both qualities can be experienced vividly. So vividly, in fact, that these qualities may even be turned upside down to become their opposites, hate and rational stupidity. But even that negative phenomena can be an opportunity. Through experiencing the painful stretching between the opposites, human beings can attain an autonomous knowledge of the essence of love and wisdom. Ultimately we can learn to embody it!

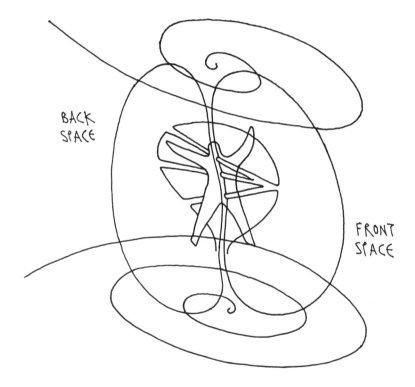

Example
The drawing shows the vertical light channel connecting the human being to the soul powers of Heaven and Earth and the three horizontal light channels through which the human being relates to its individual soul essence.

2.3 Gea — a juicy erotic woman

In our effort to understand the sacred geography of Earth we tend to forget that we are dealing with life. We objectify the living sensible body of a cosmic woman called Gea, virgin-mother of creation, rather than making love with her. We understand that people are primarily beings of consciousness and spirit. But do not forget the reality that at this moment, while I am writing and you are enjoying (hopefully) this book, we are embodied beings, capable of feeling and touching life in all its dimensions. Of what use is it to understand the intricate interlacing of the different dimensions of Gea's body, the landscape, if we did not touch her breasts? Without that experience, it is as if we are holding an empty, nicely ornamented vessel in our hands, without having drunk, without being filled and intoxicated with her wisdom.

It is all about love. It certainly helps to acquire knowledge, and we will make more efforts to do so. But our accumulated knowledge has little meaning if we forget that it represents nothing more than a spectrum of techniques about how to make love with Gea, the Earth Soul and its body, the landscape. By uniting love and knowledge we become capable of co-creating with her, and sharing life with the whole family of her beings.

If you are a man, imagine walking upon a sensitive, juicy feminine body as you move through the landscape. If you are a woman, imagine walking upon the body of a beautiful, virile man. Gea is both of them, and even more. It is simply not enough to walk upon her body. We must inevitably dive into the erotic dimension of touching her breath, her depth, her soul. (Perhaps have a look at my book *Touching the Breath of Gaia*.)

Sister Earth archetype

The ancient Mother Earth archetype in its traditional form is no longer appropriate to serve as a foundation for a new sustainable relationship between human beings and the Earth Soul. We are not children any more. We reach adulthood with the acceptance of a shared responsibility for life unfolding upon the Earth. If we are capable of producing technologies that bear the potential to destroy life upon the planet, how can we escape this responsibility?

Exercise 1
While walking through a given land-scape, move slowly and be fully present. Imagine, as you move forward, stepping deeply into the ground, beyond what is physically possible (like walking on fresh snow). Be conscious of any feelings, images or sensations that may arise.

Exercise 2
While walking through a given land-scape, move slowly and be fully present. Imagine that a double of yourself is walking in step with you, underground. With each step forward, the double is moving deeper into the earth. All the while you are moving above your double. How do you feel within your (real) body?

Once your double has moved so deeply into the Earth that you cannot follow it any longer, stop and unite with it. How do you feel now? What quality of information has your double gathered for you while walking through the Earth?

Exercise 3
While walking through a given land-scape, move slowly and be fully present. Imagine that while you walk you are carrying a double of yourself standing upon your shoulders. Be open to unexpected sensations, be centered, and be alert. After you have walked several steps, stop and let the information from your double sink down into your body. How does it feel? Then continue walking.

The urge to develop geomancy as a new, holistic science of geography is directly related to the imperative to discover and to ground within human consciousness a new kind of relationship to "Mother Earth." Here are some thoughts to consider about changing our concepts and creating a new relationship to "Sister Earth":

- What might be the difference to our individualized human soul once we recognize Gea, the Earth, as an individual soul that is consciously developing and inhabiting the material plane of reality with life? How can we human beings receive our inspirations and put them into practice, manifesting the fruits of this multidimensional partnership?

- Gea, the Earth Soul, is huge—we human beings are relatively small. Can this difference matter at the soul level, where energy or form has no known meaning? In the context of multidimensionality, we must accept in advance that any surprise is possible. In my experience, meeting such a gigantic woman as Gea can easily happen as an eye-to-eye encounter.

- We described above the creative potentials that human civilizations have brought to the Earth and its evolutions. We also discussed the benefits that the Earth can bestow upon human beings during our stay within the Earth Cosmos. There is obviously a partner relationship vibrating between us and the Earth Soul that needs to be recognized. Sister Earth is the right expression to use to honor Gea as a partner of humanity.

To a son or daughter, a mother always stays a mother. But by recognizing the Earth Soul as our partner, we are expressing our wish to renew and transform our relationship to Mother Nature, the womb that enables our birth into the material dimension, an aspect of the Earth Soul.

Example 1 depicts an Earth Soul figurine from the Palaeolithic Age, called "The Venus of Willendorf." Note how the stars on her head link her to the world of spirit and the roots anchor her in the material dimension. She is a true embodiment of the Earth Cosmos!

Example 2 shows a medieval sculpture of the Virgin with a child standing on the Moon, which bears the Mother Earth's face. Imagine that the Virgin represents Sister Earth, her son stands for humanity. Both are presented as partners relating to the ancient Mother Earth archetype that is closely associated with the cycles of the Moon.

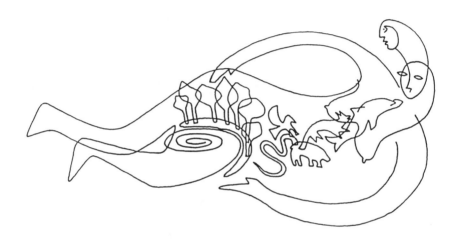

Example 3 represents the Earth Soul as a Life-Giving Goddess, as she revealed herself to me on April 19th, 1991. From her vulva as a source of life power, evolutions develop in the direction of her head. Note the position of the human head that represents human consciousness as a mirror in which Gea can obtain an overview of her entire creation. The partner relationship becomes obvious.

Example 4 illustrates my vision of the Earth Soul in Madrid on November 8, 2002, in which she showed herself as giant dancing Virgin Goddess. Gradually the features of her face took on a human character, as if she were signaling her desire to be recognized in a partnership relationship.

2.4 The holographic principle of reality

Seen from the point of view of our rational mind, reality extends around us as a multitude of phenomena, which can be classified and systemized to provide a sense of order to the environment. But how does this multitude relate to the oneness (the only One) and to the void of infinity? Imagining the multidimensional structure of reality, as described above, can help us to understand eternity pulsating within each unit of existence. A natural phenomenon is related to a specific archetype of universal creation, which is woven around an atom of infinity. But this atom of eternity is identical with all other atoms of infinity, pulsating within any of the stars, landscapes, beings or within a piece of wood. We are speaking of holographic units.

"Holon" is used in geomantic theory to denote this wonderful non-hierarchical and pan-democratic way in which the world is composed, if perceived in a pluridimensional way. Like the word "whole," "holon" is derived from an ancient Greek term representing a rounded-up unit.

If we say that a landscape is a holon for itself, we mean that the given landscape is permeated by all the dimensions needed to make it alive, to give it its sense of identity, and to anchor it at the heart of infinity. Within that landscape there exist a multitude of places that represent a holon for itself. Each of these "smaller units" is not smaller than the holon of the landscape, of which they seem to be only a part. Since each holon, no matter how small it is, is equipped with all the levels, power points and dimensions that are characteristic for the Earth, or even for the universal space, it represents a complete universe. It deserves an equal measure of attention and love as does the entire Whole. And yet, it may be only the holon of a forest or a garden. But focusing one's exploration on the holon of that forest, or garden, one can expect to find within its boundaries all the phenomena needed for the universe to exist and to function properly.

A vital-energy center (solar plexus) of a garden might be a tiny center, seeming not much more than a glowing point of power. A solar plexus center of the corresponding landscape would look like a sun shining far out into the landscape's space. The vital-energy center of an ever bigger holon, for example of a country or a continent, would radiate that much greater. And yet they all are equally important in relationship to the holon that they supply with life energy!

2.5 What could a holistic vision of the Earth be like?

A geocentric world system

As we begin to understand the holon principle, it is natural to see the Earth at the center of its own space. The so-called geocentric view of the Earth and cosmos is the only logical one. If the Earth with its cosmic environment represents a rounded-up holon, then the Earth is at the center of its own universe. Following this line of thought, I refer to the geocentric holon of our planet as "the Earth Cosmos."

The classical geocentric vision of our planet portrays the Earth at the center of the universe, with planets and stars circling around it. Translating this vision into modern language implies that the Earth is not a random phenomenon within our solar system. The Earth is a conscious presence, Gea-centered at its heart core. All other planets and the stars form the Earth's environment, and have a role to play within the wholeness of the Earth Cosmos.

This is why the classical image of the Earth holon depicts them circling around the Earth. They are shown in their relationship to the essence of the Earth and its evolution.

Of course we cannot deny that the Earth is also part of the next bigger holon, the holon of the solar system.

There the sun sits at the center, and the Earth is circling the center together with other sister and brother planets. The traditional geocentric and the scientific heliocentric world systems do not exclude but complement each other.

Over time our rational mind has eliminated the individuality of the Earth by dismissing the geocentric world view as a product of primitive traditional knowledge. The image or concept of Gea as mother-centered at the core of its own creation was eliminated. The objective, distant, non-loving relationship to the planet and its life organism became the prevailing world view and ethic.

It is critical that we address and correct this misconception in order to remedy the current destructive course of our civilization. The holographic principle of holons that complement each other can be of great help.

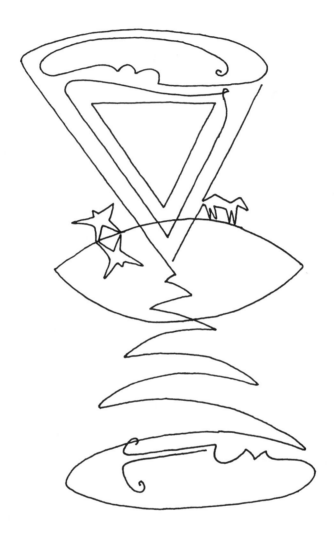

Example
A way to represent the geocentric world view, with the disc-like membrane of the Earth surface at the centre. The Earth Soul is working from the inner universe below, and the spirit of the universe from above. Note that human being finds its image mirrored in the dimension of the inner universe.

Earth mediating between the outer and the inner universe

To continue with our proposed multidimensional approach of seeing reality, we must also question the image of the Earth as a dense round ball. Understanding the Earth planet as a dense ball filled with matter, with no other life within, limits our perception to solely the material dimension of reality. However, approaching the Earth from other levels of perception can lead us to very different outcomes. Physical spaces that do not show any trace of a living organism at the material level may blossom with life of some other dimension. Traditions of many cultures worldwide regard the surrounding universe as interlaced with consciousness. We often refer to this consciousness as angelic, or perhaps divine. This consciousness represents the inner life of the Earth, be it connected to the soul presence of Gea, or to the archetypal forces that inspire the Earth creation.

Traditional cultures often speak of our reality as a "disc-like space" suspended between the inner space of the Earth and outer cosmic space. Spoken in the language of geomancy, this "disc-like space" can be compared to a holon. As an example, let's consider the holon of a landscape. The landscape appears disc-like, not only because the flat surface of the Earth belongs to its whole, but the underworld below and the spiritual atmosphere above also belong to this whole. The disc-like holon of a given landscape is composed of vital-energy streams, consciousness networks, and a multitude of pieces of solid matter. It is not a solid object—it should be understood as a permeable, multilayer membrane.

In this way each landscape of the Earth can be seen as a sensitive membrane that enables the inner soul power of the Earth to emerge from the planetary body, to expand, and to talk to the consciousness of the universe. At the same time the membrane of the Earth surface allows the soul power of the universe to enter the inner cosmos of the Earth and to interact with its inner universe. As the nexus of a continuous exchange between the inner and the outer cosmos, the surface of the Earth is capable of infusing matter with life. The alchemy of exchange between the outer universe and the inner cosmos of the Earth makes life possible!

Several different evolutions have developed within the fertile space of the Earth membrane, among them humankind. Yet we may stall in our evolution as long as the exchange between Heaven and Earth (the inner and the outer universe of the Earth holon) continues to be blocked through the collective thought form that depicts the inner Earth as a solid ball of matter and the outer universe as a dead space. One of the tasks of a new geomancy as sacred geography is to provide human consciousness with the imagination and tools to transform this dominant thought form.

Where to locate the otherworld?

As long as the Earth is visualized as a solid ball of matter and the outer universe as an empty space, we have no place to locate our dead. We can bury or burn their corpses, but where do we search for and find the souls of our beloved friends and relatives? Is there any other culture besides our modern materialistic one that denies the existence of some kind of afterlife? However, if one starts to comprehend each unit of the Earth surface as an autonomous multidimensional holon, the situation changes drastically.

We can imagine the disc-like holon of a given landscape as the space within which materialized forms of life evolve. Human beings as eternal souls incarnate within the disc-like holon of a specific landscape to enjoy physical life forms. We enjoy them from the moment of birth until the moment of death. But where do we come from, where do we go to, and how do we exist beyond that relatively short time span?

Let's regard the disc-like membrane of the material world as surrounded by a large aura. This membrane and aura can be understood as a vast etheric (non-physical) space organism. Within this space organism there are different ambiences or frequencies that are provided for human souls to pulsate and evolve during the time when we are not incarnated in human bodies. It is this etheric space organism, surrounding the materialized world, that we call the "otherworld." Since different extensions of the otherworld are positioned all around the physical world, we generally perceive them to be either "below" the ground or floating high "above" our heads in the universe. We speak traditionally of a duality that locates purgatory in the underworld below and paradise in heaven above. But we should not project prejudices upon these two polarities of "below" and "above," which have been separated due to a framework of consciousness that has lost a sense of the whole.

According to my experience each of the two otherworld ambiences has a different role to fulfill. There are etheric environments needed for souls that just have left their incarnation period behind. They need to become accustomed to being in a body-less state. They may need to process their earthly experiences and purify some sequences by experiencing them again. Usually these kinds of ambiences are located in the area of the underworld "below."

Other human souls that are accustomed to being in the etheric aura of the Earth may wish to help their sisters and brothers struggling with the challenges of the physical world. They gather in etheric centers that connect their activity to those souls incarnated on the Earth surface who are in resonance with a given task or way of thinking. We usually locate such soul centers in the atmosphere "above," even if some of them work from the underworld "below."

2.6 The co-creative role of some parallel evolutions

Animals and elemental beings

If we look closer at the evolution of human beings we discover that this evolution is composed of two parallel strands. On the one side there are human beings walking the Earth in solid, physical bodies. On the other side we encounter soul beings, free of any form, encircling the physical Earth space. These two strands of human evolution lose their meaning if they are not involved in an intense interaction. (See the previous chapter.)

A similar dual pattern can also be applied to some other evolutions that occupy the disc-like membrane of the Earth surface. Let's first consider the relationship between the evolution of elemental beings (environmental spirits) and animal evolution. There is no relationship between them if we acknowledge only the conventional scientific point of view. The whole range of animal species can be experienced in zoological gardens or studied in scientific books. Our rational minds have no problem with that. However, elemental beings do not appear in materialized forms. They are invisible, not comprehensible to rational consciousness, and are considered nonexistent.

But through a pluridimensional way of perception, nature and environmental spirits can appear as part of one and the same reality that they share with animals. Even if no physical forms are evident, these beings may be perceived as a presence, perhaps as a specific emotional quality of an ambience. It may even be possible to distinguish their different roles in the landscape and the etheric configuration of their light bodies.

In the course of gathering more experience about the presence of elemental beings, we discover that their world is structured in a similar way to that of the animal world. We can describe several examples. Compared to micro-organisms at the lowest stage of animal evolution, there are tiny elemental beings, providing consciousness to rocks, soil, or water drops. Traditionally they are called "minutes." In the course of evolving toward more complex forms, animals made efforts to adapt to the archetypal four elements and to develop corresponding strands of evolution. Some animals specialized in the direction of the water element, like fish; others developed to interact with the airy space, like birds; and others evolved to walk on the earth.

Since elemental beings are not attached to form, they are capable of embodying the four elements archetype more fully than animals. There are consciousness units, traditionally called "nymphs" or "nixes" which direct energies of life within the water element. We use the term "fairies" to refer to beings that work with atmospheric space and its cycles (the air element). The consciousness aspect of nature that works on translating life energy into form is usually associated with earth elemental beings, called "gnomes." In addition, elemental beings are free to move within the element of fire, which the animal evolution does not include. Spirits of transmutation and those who carry or transmit inspiration are associated with the fire element.

Although they have developed along a similar pattern, the evolutions of elemental beings and animals are essentially different. The role of elemental beings is to dive again and again deep "down" into the soul consciousness of the Earth (Gea). From there they bring impulses to the Earth surface that are directing and modeling all the different life processes on the physical level. Their evolution has brought forth all the variations of elemental beings and nature spirits needed in order to reach and connect with every single life form, from vast landscapes to the tiny sand corn. (For specifics on the evolution of environmental consciousness see my book *Nature Spirits and Elemental Beings*.)

On the other hand, animals are cosmic beings incarnated on the Earth. The archetypal souls of different species, called "group souls," incarnate as different animal species upon the Earth surface. But basically they do not belong to the Earth, but to the soul dimension of the universe. The Zodiac, the circle of sacred animals embodied in different star systems, stands as a symbol for the cosmic origin of animal evolution. (For more details about animal evolution see my book *The Daughter of Gaia*.)

Swimming, crawling and navigating through the space of the Earth surface, animals are distributing different cosmic qualities and performing energy work that is essential for the life quality of the Earth's ecosphere. Without their contribution, brought to the Earth from different star systems, the Earth Cosmos could not move forward along its evolutionary path. Thus these two other evolutions, one bringing the impulses from the core of the Earth and one from the vastness of the universe, are complementing each other in their endeavor to enrich the life of the planet.

Environmental spirits and plants

Compared with animals, plants are beings of the Earth. Plants represent an evolution brought forth by the Earth Soul, its archetypes and its nature spirits. This does not mean that the plant world is lacking spiritual dimension. One should remember our discussion about the inner cosmos of the Earth and its different layers. Plants may not express the spirituality of the star cosmos, as animals do, but they definitely express the wisdom of the inner universe of the Earth. To be able to express the soul powers of Gea, the Earth Virgin, plants require a consciousness to mediate between the archetypes stored inside the Earth and upon the Earth surface (where plants grow). Nature spirits represent this mediating consciousness.

So we have three levels of plant life and two evolutions involved with plant life:

- The physical level of plant life is known to our five senses, and studied and described in detail by physical science.

- The deepest level of plant life refers to cosmic archetypes that lend specific spiritual qualities to different plant species. Usually we use the Sanskrit expression "Deva," meaning divine beings, to denote these soul beings that embody plant archetypes. Devas can be understood as angels of the Earth Cosmos.

- Nature spirits and elemental beings mediate between the two extremes. Their task is to guide the growth of each single plant according to the master pattern provided by the Deva of the given species. Different kinds of elemental beings may work on one and the same plant. Elemental beings of the Earth Element are responsible for form development, fire spirits for the ripening of fruits, and fairies (beings of the air element) for cycles of growth and the colors of flowers.

Exercise 1

Choose a plant, possibly a vegetable or a wild plant. Bow down close to the plant or kneel down beside it. Be peaceful, and present. Imagine moving with your attention toward the plant, while at the same time the plant is moving toward you. Perhaps repeat the movement a few times. Then forget about the exercise, and quickly open yourself to any perceptions you may receive.

Exercise 2

The objective of this exercise is to perceive all three dimensions of plant life through the flower. Choose a flower, come close to it, and observe its beauty, carefully and in detail (the physical level). Imagine entering the space of the flower like a hovering bee. While remaining inside the flower, turn around to perceive its inner colors and qualities (the level of flower fairy). Still maintaining your attention inside the flower, imagine bouncing yourself over to make a full loop. Now you will find yourself on the devic level, the level of the plant archetype. Be open to impressions from this moment. Then return to yourself, fully grounded, eyes wide open. Choose another type of flower for another exploration.

2.7 The human body as a map of the Earth Cosmos

The holographic principle according to which the Earth Cosmos is structured can help us to understand the specific role of human beings in relation to sacred geography. As with earth landscapes, we perceive human beings as pluridimensional. Let us consider a human being as the sum total of our material body, etheric structure, consciousness extensions, soul essence and our divine core. As a holon a human being represents the smallest unit of the Earth Cosmos. In other words, a human being embodies a holographic image of the Earth's whole. As a result—and this insight is of central importance in geomancy—it is possible to interpret a landscape in the mirror of our own body.

Traditionally the human skeleton is said to correspond to the mineral layers of the Earth. One can also compare the veins that carry our blood to the rivers and streams of the landscape. Different life processes in the landscape can be seen as corresponding to various functions of human organs. This correspondence on the material level has a more or less symbolic quality. Much more important to us, however, is the correspondence on the etheric level between the human body and the landscape. It is here that the human mind generally lacks the capability to provide comprehensive geomantic interpretations of the vital-energy phenomena behind the scenery of a given landscape.

Chakra systems of the human body compared to the landscape

Different vital-energy centers of the landscape can be compared to the chakras of the human body. Vital-energy streams, like ley-lines, flow similarly to the energy flow of human acupuncture meridians. "Acupuncture meridians" are tiny energy channels located throughout the body with the task of distributing vital life force throughout the body, a task that ley-lines perform in a given landscape. "Chakras" are usually understood as etheric centers scattered throughout the human light body. Their role is to concentrate certain powers or qualities and to radiate them out into our personal energy fields.

To compare the etheric centers of the human body with those of the landscape we need to challenge the prevailing dominance of the so-called "seven-chakra system" that has been adopted by the

Western mind. To a clairvoyant person the holon of another human being looks like a universe full of shining stars. They represent different chakras distributed throughout the human body and its aura. As there are different star constellations in the sky, the seven-chakra system is only one of many different constellations of chakras within the human holon. Certainly the seven-chakra system is an important one, and can well represent the different levels of the human being positioned between Earth below and cosmos above.

This role of the seven-chakra ladder is apparent if we observe a human being in a standing position. But if we lie down on our back, we can assume that there must be another system of chakras operating within the Earth and Heaven relationship. I refer to this as a "system of horizontal light channels." These channels connect the chakras at the back of our body with those at the front. The horizontal lines of chakras, always aligned in three in a line, exist at least at the level of the sexual chakra (or hara), the heart, and the chakra of the third eye. (For details see my book *Turned Upside Down*.)

In both cases we have chakra constellations that show different chakras aligned along linear light channels, vertical and horizontal. This may provoke a sensation in a given landscape of chakras (vital-energy centers) similarly appearing along straight lines. However, it is actually very rare that the vital-energy centers of a landscape holon would appear aligned along certain axes. This may happen in a narrow valley landscape, along a river, or along a mountain ridge. It may also be a consequence of a human projection, for example designing portions of a landscape along certain lines, as in the case of a park alley. Usually vital-energy centers (chakras of the Earth surface) are scattered randomly throughout the landscape, just as stars are scattered in the sky.

Within the human holon we can also find chakra constellations that do not follow a linear order. For example, let's consider the chakra system corresponding to the four elements. The chakras of the fire element are to be found on the ear lobes, shoulders, and hips. Concerning the earth element chakras, one should look for them at the elbows, behind the knees, and (for a fifth one) between the knees. Air element chakras are found on the feet, palms of the hands, and one above the head. Finely, the two water element chakras pulsate above both breasts and at the sides along the line encircling the heart center.

If you stand in the "Leonardo da Vinci position" with your hands raised above your head, it is possible to understand or experience that the four element chakras are forming four circular constellations.

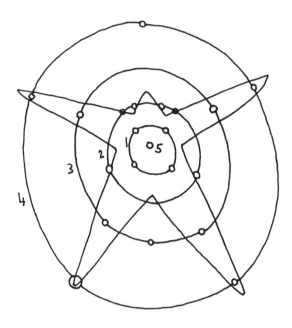

Example
The drawing depicts the system of the four elements chakras placed in a circular way around the heart centre (5): element water chakras (1), element fire chakras (2), element earth chakras (3), element air chakras (4).

Organs of the human body compared to landscape organs

We do not need to depend on correspondences to human chakra systems while searching for a language to interpret different places and qualities within a landscape. We can also base our interpretations upon correspondences with different body organs.

Let's take our skin as a first example. The function of our skin can be compared to the function of the holon membrane of a place or landscape. A holon membrane protects the autonomy of the given place and serves as a medium of communication between different spatial units. The same is literally true about the function of our skin. Kidneys are not only responsible for cleaning of body fluids. Chinese medicine honors them as the main source of vital potential within the human body. Similarly, there are places in the landscape that are rich with sources of archetypal powers emanating from the core of the Earth. Often they are connected to water streams, but not necessarily. Their role is to hold the vital potential of the given place in a fluid state.

The navel represents another important aspect of the landscape. It represents the spiritual center of a given place. The ancient Greeks spoke about the navel of the world, the so-called "omphalos," as central to a specific landscape—not only because the navel represents the exact central point of the human body, but also because the navel marks the place where the human embryo is fed by the vital energies of the mother. If we compare a mother's role to the role that Gea, the Earth Soul, performs for the life processes at the Earth's surface, we can sense the kind of geomantic meaning that navel-like places perform in the landscape.

The heart organ is another example. The importance that the "fire of the heart" has for the whole organism cannot be overemphasized. Pumping the blood to each and every distant corner of the body to provide for its regeneration is a powerful symbol that finds a correspondence in the heart center of any landscape. In addition, recent scientific research indicates that the heart possesses its own brain. In geomantic terms, a heart center pulsating in the landscape can also have a spiritual function. Chinese medicine further connects the function of the heart with human speech, inspiring further exploration about how the heart center of a place functions in relationship to creative processes in the given landscape.

Finally, we should not forget about sexual organs. They have a clear correspondence in the Yin-Yang system of the landscape, which relates to the polarity of vital energies. We can also consider how the feminine and masculine are manifested through differently shaped landscape forms. Going deeper, we find that human sexual activity finds correspondence in the way the archetypal powers of the Earth Soul move through the landscape in the form of dragon paths.

PART III

EARTH COSMOS — GEOMANTIC PHENOMENA

3.1 Auric fields of places and landscapes

BEFORE WE START to look at the different geomantic phenomena appearing at the surface of the Earth membrane, I ask the reader not to expect to be given a definitive list. It is hard to believe the extent to which Mother Nature and her grandmother, the Earth Soul, are such creative beings. Look at the extraordinary variety of plants growing all over the Earth! There are not only billions of species, but each particular plant is in some way uniquely shaped.

Like the thick layer of atmosphere enveloping the planet at the physical level, energy fields composed of vital powers, emotional consciousness clouds, and spiritual impulses are winding and pulsing around the globe. Different layers of physical atmosphere, planetary electromagnetic fields, and different components of etheric aura complement one another. Together they represent the subtle womb within which are nourished and protected different continents, landscapes, and places of the Earth.

Auric fields of places and landscapes may be compared to the immune system of the human body. They hold and protect the individual essence and vital organism of each given holon, maintaining autonomy and integrity. Keeping our discussion on the holographic principle in mind, it should not be difficult to understand that not only is the planet as a whole bathing in its auric fields, but also each place or landscape separately within it. Smaller holon-units float within bigger ones, like spheres within a sphere. Within the aura of a continent there are many landscapes surrounded by their own aura-spheres. Within each of those landscapes, there are a multitude of places surrounded by their own smaller aura-spheres. Within those places there are many minute ambiences surrounded by their own even smaller aura-spheres, such as individual human beings, trees, and animals.

Four element fields — the vital aura of a place or landscape

Compared with the physical (chemical, thermal) atmosphere that covers a landscape or place above its surface, the etheric aura surrounding a place is in the form of a sphere. Half of the auric sphere extends above the Earth surface, and the other half pulsates below the surface. The vital aura of a place or landscape creates the conditions for life on the Earth surface to flourish, die, and be reborn. To be a source of the bio-potentials of a place on all different levels, the sphere of the vital aura is composed of the energies of the four elements (earth, water, air, and fire) lifted to the level of the fifth element, the ethers. To say it in another way, the auric sphere of a place is composed of earthly etheric fields, fields of humid ether, airy etheric fields, and diverse focuses of fiery ether.

1. *Earthly etheric fields* are composed of basic vital energies emanating from the depth of the Earth. They originate from within the core of the planet. Levitating toward its surface, they concentrate at first within the subterranean half-sphere of the aura. Like ground water at the physical level, the "sea" of the earth ether is permeating the underground space representing a factor of stability for the life streams and processes on the surface of the given place or landscape. Through mineral layers, rocks, forests, and other biological phenomena, the earth ether penetrates the surface skin of the landscape, rising sometimes as high as a human being's figure does—but not more. Its power stays concentrated within the ground.

2. *Fields of humid ether* have the task of carrying and distributing life forces (bio-energy) throughout the landscape so that each living being can take part in its potentials. This is why fields of watery ethers are perceived as organic streams moving back and forth through the spherical holon of a place, like rivers or oceanic streams, usually without any fixed order. There are macro-streams following the main features of the given landscape and a multitude of micro-streams approaching singular spots, like trees, caves, rocks, or springs. The intensity of fluid ether streams moving throughout a place reflects the level of life quality of that location.

3. *Airy etheric powers* are concentrated within the envelope of a given holon. Within the membrane of a holon's sphere is the mental wealth

of the place, the memories and knowledge needed to secure its existence. The life of the landscape draws forth information needed from the membrane, which is available to the elemental beings piloting the life of the place. This phenomenon is associated not only with the holon membrane of a landscape but also with the spherical membranes of each separate place, each rock, each plant, and other living beings within that landscape. As a result, at this level the landscape looks like a silvery ball filled with smaller balls that in turn are full of even smaller silvery balls.

4. *Focuses of fiery* ethers are distributed throughout the landscape according to its chakra system, the flow of its ley-lines, and the positioning of other vital-energy phenomena within the landscape's organism. All individual geomantic phenomena in a given landscape represent different focuses of the fire element. The fiery ether is a carrier of impulses into the holon of the landscape, usually transmitted through some form of radiation. Detecting a strong source of fiery ethers may be a sign that we have come across one of the chakras (vital-energy centers) of the place. Detecting a line of fiery ether may be a sign to search there for a ley-line.

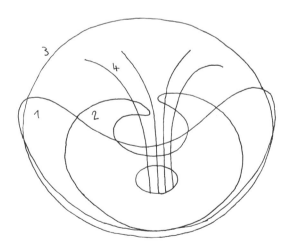

Example
This drawing illustrates how the four elements energy fields are distributed within the city space of Wiesbaden, Germany (1 – earth field, 2 – water field, 3 – air field, 4 – fire field).

Emotional fields of places and landscapes

The vital aura of places and landscapes is related to the life forces of a place. This vital aura is permeated with another, more refined auric field. This more refined field is an expression of consciousness as it resonates throughout a landscape's holon. Since the consciousness of nature and the elemental world is emotional it involves colors and qualities rather than energies. The emotional aura is sometimes also called the "astral" aura.

To understand how emotional fields come into being, one should imagine a landscape populated with elemental beings and other environmental spirits. These beings and spirits produce a kind of fluid that can be called an "emotional aura." The aura permeates the landscape with the archetypal information needed by the beings to be connected to the soul essence of Gea and, most of all, to continuously feel the loving care of the Earth Soul. The landscape is constantly being bathed in the colors and qualities of its emotional aura, which we perceive on the physical level as the glowing beauty of its nature.

There are vast crowds of simple elemental beings in the landscape producing its emotional aura, for example elves working with different types of plants. At the same time there are also powerful intelligence focuses, like Devas of a particular landscape, that provide individual coloring to the emotional aura of that specific place.

Holon and membrane systems

The separation or division of individual holon units within a landscape is essential for that landscape to retain its multidimensional essence. To this end there are borders or invisible walls that divide autonomous spheres of individual spaces one from another. In some cases such an invisible mantle is called a "coat of protection."

Sensing such a "wall" within a specific place means that one has discovered the border of its energy field surrounded by its membrane. It is important to understand that such border structures in their natural appearance are always transparent. These membranes make communication between different holon units possible. There is a clear division of holon units and yet a vivid exchange. This is a precondition for the immune system of a holon to work properly.

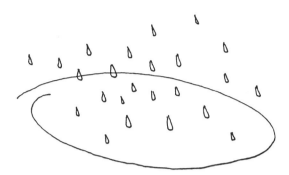

Example 1
Let us consider the example of the emotional aura of the moor extending south of the Slovenian capital, Ljubljana. Even though today it is mainly dry the whole landscape is still governed by a mighty water being, a landscape nymph that is preserving the watery quality of that landscape. As a consequence the whole atmosphere of the Ljubljana moor is permeated by silvery water-like drops. They are an expression of the nymph's presence within the atmosphere of that holon. Although invisible, they lend the landscape a sacred feeling.

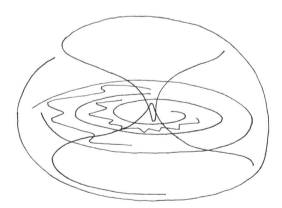

Example 2
Eberharting is a forgotten sacred place in Bavaria where a Montessori school now flourishes. The main quality of the holon can be expressed as Heaven kissing the Earth. As a result of this union the holon of the corresponding landscape is impregnated with mandala-like structures that appear in ruby-red shades of color.

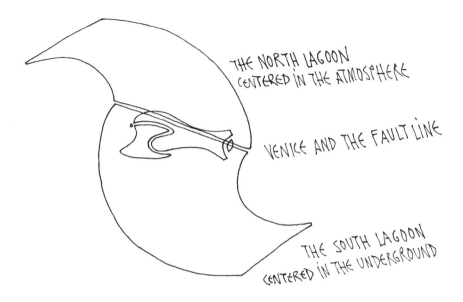

THE NORTH LAGOON
CENTERED IN THE ATMOSPHERE

VENICE AND THE FAULT LINE

THE SOUTH LAGOON
CENTERED IN THE UNDERGROUND

Example 3
The Venice lagoon is my third example. The city of Venice is positioned
at the center of a lagoon so that it divides the holon of the lagoon into
a northern and a southern part. The division is clearly felt as a kind of
an energetic fault line that runs along the back of the Venetian "fish."
(The city shows a fish form.) The emotional quality of the northern
part of the Venice lagoon is centered in the atmosphere and is bright
and shiny. The lovely islands of Torcello, Burano, and Murano are an
expression of this bright atmospheric quality.

The power of the southern half of the lagoon is centered under-
ground. Little attention has been given to this area. Its quality feels
rather dark and heavy, even if the landscape is not very different than
that of the northern half.

The role of the "fault line" is to enable communication between
both parts of the lagoon. The exchange of atmospheric and under-
ground qualities looks like waves moving back and forth. Important
Venetian churches like Madonna dell Orto, San Francesco della Vigna,
and San Pietro di Castello are positioned along this line.

Two possible kinds of problems can occur. Due to some destructive pressure a membrane might be broken. There now is an energy leak that weakens the given place. A healing work may be needed to restore the immune system of that place. It is also possible that the membrane of a place or person is closed too much. This may be done intentionally to strengthen the protective role of the membrane. However, the exchange between different levels of holon can then become impaired or stuck. In this case we need to find the reason for the exaggerated need for protection in order to solve the problem.

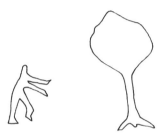

Exercise 1
Pick out a tree and ensure that you are far enough from it. Concentrate on the essence of that tree as you slowly approach it. With the palms of your hands, try to feel when you bump into the tree's holon membrane. Try the exercise with another tree, or repeat the exercise with a glass of water or a piece of a mineral.

Exercise 2
Obtain a geographical map of a landscape that you have already experienced. Tune to the essence of that landscape through the map. Then with your hands slowly go over the map and feel where the holon borders of different places are located. Observe how they intersect. Try to feel their spherical forms.

What about geomantic grids and other dowsing phenomena?

During the last few decades dowsers have developed different languages to interpret their findings. However, one should not necessarily connect these interpretations with the multidimensional reality of a given place. Why? In most cases dowsers are exclusively bound or tied to findings made with different kinds of dowsing instruments. Dowsing instruments are always connected to certain mental structures that serve as a medium of perception and interpretation. This means that geomantic phenomena are undergoing a considerable process of mental digestion or cogitation. This does not mean that dowser's findings are of no value. Their language simply needs to be understood and translated, if needed, into one's own way of understanding the space of reality.

For example, let's consider the linear rectangular structures that dowsers often find. They may be called "Hartman" or "Cury" grids. I believe they represent regular rhythms of pulsation within the vital-energy field of a place interpreted in a specific way. By detecting distortions in the structure of those grids, it is possible to find causes for problems associated with people living in a particular place. But there are other ways to deal with the same problem. One can, for example, examine the quality of the auric fields of the given place through avenues of immediate perception.

During the last decade dowsing has made great progress. It is possible to dowse etheric phenomena and explore formations of Earth chakras, ley-lines and other phenomena without experiencing them subjectively. Dowsing can be used as a complement to immediate perception of invisible phenomena in the landscape, but one must be aware of the language used.

Example
An example of comparative research using two different languages to interpret the same phenomena, undertaken with the dowser and my fellow artist Peter Straus, is published in my book Nature Spirits and Elemental Beings *(Chapter 6).*

3.2 Centers of vital power — Earth chakras

The first chapter on geomantic phenomena deals with phenomena that touch the landscape as a whole body, for example vital-energy fields. Now we move forward to examine different sources of powers which, once generated, constitute the vital-energy fields of a given landscape. We shall examine Earth chakras as sources from which the vital aura of places and landscapes draws its strength and ability to sustain life. We will use the expression "Earth chakras" as an alternative for "centers of vital power," and in many cases use similarities to human body chakras to explain the functioning of corresponding vital-energy centers of places and landscapes.

Breathing systems

The breathing system is a basic component of vital-energy systems. For the landscape, as with human and other embodied beings, breathing is essential to life. It is a system polarized between two phases, breathing in and breathing out. In the landscape breathing serves as an exchange between the atmospheric and the underground halves of its holon. Circling between the atmospheric and underground spaces, life forces of a given place are going through a constant cycle of recharging and regeneration.

Let's begin the description of the cycle with the outbreath. A center of outbreath looks like a hole in the etheric tissue of the Earth surface. Through the hole of the outbreath center fresh vital energies are constantly pouring into the atmospheric space of the given holon. They expand within the atmospheric half of the holon to permeate all landscape structures and beings of the Earth surface with refreshed vital power and information.

The center of inbreath also appears like a hole in the etheric tissue of the Earth surface. Vital powers of the atmospheric half of the given holon are constantly being drawn in and distributed within the underground half of the holon's sphere.

Dark like a night's darkness, the ambience of the underground is a place of rest and regeneration. Vital energies arriving underground through the pull of the inbreath center experience renewal there, and the information gathered at the Earth surface is distributed. The peace of the dark side of landscape's holon allows them to regenerate and to return to their primordial state of neutrality.

Through the breathing hole of the outbreath center the neutralized and regenerated powers will be distributed again throughout the atmospheric half of the holon. But the landscape is not breathing rhythmically like animals and human beings. The flow of the in- and outbreath stream is constant. Two separate breathing centers are required, one for the constant flow of outbreath and the other for the uninterrupted flow of inbreath. The breathing system is a basic vital-energy system. Both breathing centers are found on all holon levels, be it in a small room or garden, or within the holon of a place, a landscape, a continent or the Earth globe as whole.

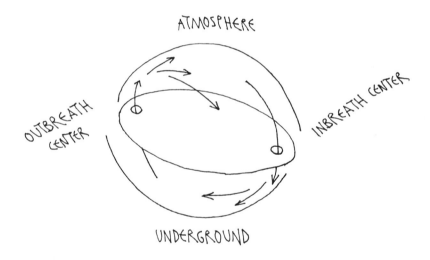

Example 1
Usually both breathing centers are found in two separate locations within the given holon.

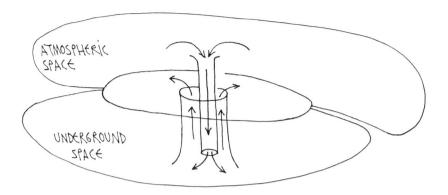

Example 2
There are exceptions to the rule described above. On the grounds of the community and peace center Tamera, close to Colos in Portugal, for the first time I discovered a breathing center that shows a united in- and outbreath. Later I found a few more. At the center of the chakra there is an etheric channel through which the stream of inbreath flows. It is surrounded by a ring-like opening embracing the channel through which the outbreath stream is pouring out into the atmosphere of the place.

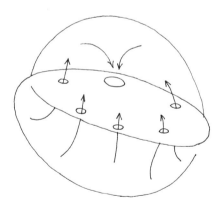

Example 3
Sometimes, as in the case of large breathing systems of regions and continents, the breathing system is composed of one central inbreath chakra. Outbreath is performed by a number of outbreath centers located in a circular or half-circular form around the inbreath center.

Centers of grounding

It may be hard to understand that the landscape needs centers of grounding. The landscape itself is an expression of the Earth essence—so why does it need to be grounded?

Through the development of different, relative autonomous evolutions of life forms on the Earth surface a strong levitating wave of energy is being unleashed. Life wants to explode and be distributed throughout the universe. To produce a counterforce and balance to this kind of energy, centers of grounding are needed at each level of the holon. They represent gravitational forces pulling life downwards toward the center of the Earth.

Centers of grounding can be compared with the lowest of the seven chakras positioned along the human spine, called the "root chakra." The primary task of this chakra is to hold the human being rooted within the core of the Earth. The root chakra works as a counterbalance to the mental energy focussed in our head, which is an energy that can drive us in all directions, following ideas that often are not well-grounded.

Similar challenges of grounding confront modern civilization. We alter the landscape and build cities without connecting their structure to the energy organism of the underlying landscape, a problem exacerbated by the flash-like rapidity of mental processes rushing through the city structures. As a result the roots of life are being pulled out and nature has great difficulty infusing human culture with the needed life forces. The grounding centers of the city landscape must be strengthened to introduce needed healing processes.

Yin-Yang systems

The polarization of feminine and masculine poles is needed to create the enfolding of life from generation to generation—within both the human family and the landscape. To foster creative processes in the landscape, centers are needed where life energies become Yin-Yang, feminine-masculine polarized.

The Yin-Yang systems of landscape can be compared to the second chakra of the system following the human spine from the coccyx upwards, the so-called "sexual chakra." Be aware that the landscape is feminine and masculine at the same time. Therefore there always

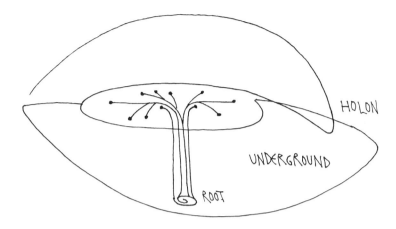

Example 1
Usually the root chakra of a place looks like a tunnel reaching verti-
cally down deep into the Earth. There, within the earth, the center
connects upwards toward different points of the landscape above,
holding them anchored in the eye of the center.

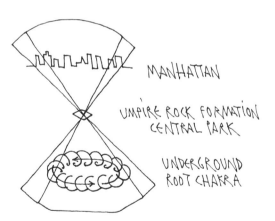

Example 2
The grounding system of Manhattan, New York, is very special. The
dangerous upsurge of the busy Manhattan spin is being counterbal-
anced deep underground by an intricate grounding center system com-
posed of a moving circle of whirlpools. The surface focus of the system
can be found in Central Park at the center of the Umpire Rock forma-
tion, not far from Columbus Circle.

exists within a holon a Yin and a Yang center, if not also their balancing pole, the neutral chakra. Yin and Yang centers represent vital-energy organs translating neutral life force into polarized energy. These centers belong to the etheric dimension of the holon. By contrast, the Yin-quality of the water system in a landscape and the Yang-quality of rocks and mountains refer to the geological structure of the landscape, not the etheric dimension.

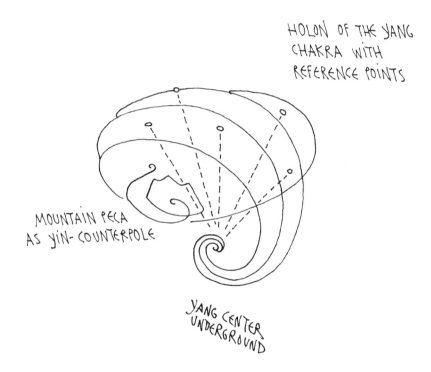

HOLON OF THE YANG CHAKRA WITH REFERENCE POINTS

MOUNTAIN PECA AS YIN-COUNTERPOLE

YANG CENTER UNDERGROUND

Example 1
Yin and Yang chakras of regions and continents are so vast that they represent a holon by themselves. This means that they include their counterpart: a major Yin chakra may have in its vicinity a minor Yang balancing center, and vice versa. I know the Yang chakra of the European continent very well, since I did a lithopuncture project in that location. The Yang chakra pulsates in the border region between Slovenia and Austrian Carinthia, centered at Bleiburg. The chakra body forms a circle 15 miles in diameter. Mount Peca at the southern edge of the chakra represents its Yin counterpole.

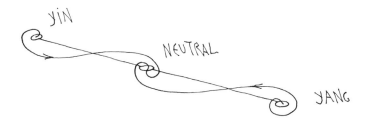

Example 2
The Yin and Yang and neutral centers are often positioned along one axis. The neutral center pulsates in the middle between the two polarized power centers. The role of the neutral center is to provide both polarized centers with neutral life energy needed for the polarization process. Energy spirals connect both polarized centers with the neutral chakra and serve as transporters.

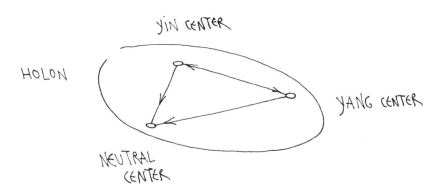

Example 3
The Yin and Yang sources in the landscape, along with the neutral center, may form a triangle extending through a given place. The three centers exchange their energies along the sides of the triangle. To the inner eye they look like rounded, mandala-like structures woven into the etheric field of the place. Within this structure the transformation (polarizing) of life force (prana) into either Yin or Yang qualities takes place. Yin powers emanating from there usually have a horizontal, rather dark, and dispersed character. Yang powers are those of light character and of fierce movement.

Vital-energy centers

Vital-energy centers are of greatest importance for the life quality of a landscape. They represent the source of fresh life force emanating from the core of the Earth. Related to the human chakra system, vital-energy centers are also called "solar plexus" centers. Like the sun, which is constantly radiating its life-giving power across the solar system, a vital-energy center is distributing etheric life information (life force) across a given place or landscape. Because of their basic importance, vital-energy centers are found at every level of holon, including the micro-holon of a room or a garden.

A primary function of a solar plexus center is to draw primeval energy from the depth of the Earth. The second function of this chakra is to transform the "raw" primeval energy into the kind of life force that can be absorbed and digested by the landscape organism and the different beings inhabiting it. The chakra of a vital-energy center is located sometimes within the Earth and sometimes at the surface. The third function of the landscape solar plexus is to distribute the transformed life-energy throughout a given place or landscape. This happens through a radiation or fountain-like dispersion.

There also is a fourth function of vital-energy centers, which does not appear within holons that are smaller than a place within a landscape. From each vital-energy chakra a circle of ley-lines emanates from the center, following the surface of the landscape. They are usually woven from two etheric lines. The whole composition of the ley-line is not wider than 1.5 meters. I call ley-lines emanating from vital-energy centers "connecting lines" because they always connect a vital-energy center with a certain point within the holon of another solar plexus center. There are usually 5 to 9 connecting lines radiating from each center. Each vital-energy center is connected to 5-9 other holons to exchange information, thus creating a network across landscapes and continents, balancing the whole geomantic system and nourishing the landscape with vital powers.

Heart centers

As in the human world, the heart center plays a special role within the landscape organism. In the same way that the human heart center

Example 1
This drawing shows a typical vital-energy center with six connecting ley-lines emanating from it. A kind of solar disc pulsates at its center.

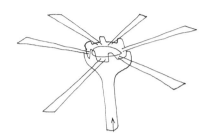

Example 2
Some vital-energy centers seem to be partly nourished from the atmosphere. The drawing shows such a center located at Eberharting in Bavaria. It is a source of five connecting lines.

Example 3
The drawing shows the vital-energy center of the Findhorn community in Scotland, with the solar plexus disc in the middle and five emanating connection leys. It is positioned at the side of the Community Center, centered in the laurel bush in the herb garden.

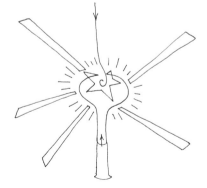

shows different levels of functions, the heart systems of places can be very diverse in their function and constitution. The human heart center plays an important role in regard to one's vitality, as well as one's balance between the cosmos and the Earth, especially on spiritual and emotional levels. The heart center of a landscape also plays an important role at the vital-energy level. It functions as a chakra of renewal. It draws in depleted vital forces and regenerates them by bringing them into contact with the infinity that is anchored at the core of each heart center. A touch of eternity is enough to bring powers of life instantly back to their pristine status. Poetically we say that at the core of each heart glows a divine spark.

Each heart center must be connected to the core of the Earth and to the spiritual dimension of the universal holon in order to link life forces with infinity. In maintaining the connection between two cosmic holons, the one of the Earth and that of the wider universe, another role of the heart center becomes evident. The heart center maintains balance between the microcosmic holon of the Earth and the macro-cosmos of the vast universe. The heart chakra maintains balance between Earth and Heaven.

The life forces that have been drawn into the heart chakra for renewal must be distributed back to the etheric space of the corresponding holon. This is how the characteristic two-beat rhythm of a heart center functions: drawing-in is succeeded by distributing out. Contraction is followed by expansion.

Finally, there is something about heart centers that cannot be properly explained. A heart center touches one deeply because of its combined emotional and spiritual levels. I believe that it is the presence of Gea, the Earth Soul, the Earth Virgin and Mother, that expresses its love for each single particle of her creation through a heart center, be it the heart of a human, animal or landscape.

There is a special network of heart centers embracing the Earth sphere. This network includes the tiny heart centers of single places, the heart centers of landscapes, and powerful heart centers of regions. They have no linear connections between themselves, like vital-energy centers. They have a code that connects all of them, through the means of resonance, into one heart organism of the Earth. This all-embracing heart system enables the Blue Planet to become a planet of love.

Example 1
Let's look first at the exquisite heart center of Quito, Ecuador. It is located within a sacred hill positioned at the city's center that Indios call "*Chungoloma*" (Hill of the Heart), and that Spaniards call "*Pan-ecillio.*" It shows a very strong connection to Heaven and Earth.

Example 2
The heart center at Heldenstein, Bavaria, shows the typical etheric form of a heart center. The ball at its core represents the mysterious place of contacting infinity. It is surrounded by a spiral that works two ways: it draws in powers for renewal and distributes them out into the landscape.

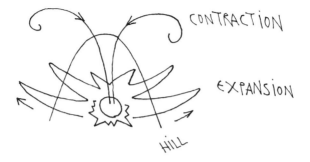

Example 3
The heart center of the Mesara landscape, near Kamares, Crete, is composed in a similar way. It is located within a symmetrically shaped hill positioned in the midst of a mountain valley. The streams of concentrating and distributing life energies are clearly expressed.

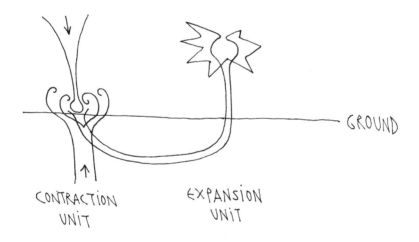

Example 4
Sometimes heart centers are composed of two units positioned close to one another. They complement each other. Such is the double heart center of Bleiburg, Austria. The unit that concentrates energies attracted for regeneration is positioned at the ground. Its complement, distributing renewed powers in the landscape, is located in the air, about 8 meters above the ground. Both units are connected through an underground channel. The first unit maintains the Earth-Cosmos connection.

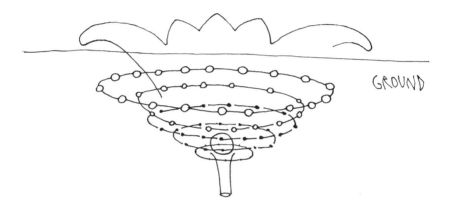

GROUND

Example 5
Here is an exquisite example of a heart center I discovered among the ruins of the Greek town Aphrodisias in Asia Minor, dedicated to Aphrodite, the Goddess of Love. It is located below the former Aphrodite pilgrimage temple that was later turned into a Christian basilica.

The heart center is positioned underground and looks like a circular amphitheater. Each level of the "amphitheater" is composed of a ring of light balls rotating around the center, a golden ball of the heart sphere. Rhythmically an impulse arrives from the core of the Earth to activate the amphitheater-like composition. After being activated the heart energy blossoms up to spill the love of Gea into the surrounding landscape.

The nature of this heart center has been obviously mutilated by the ritual activity of pilgrims coming there century after century.

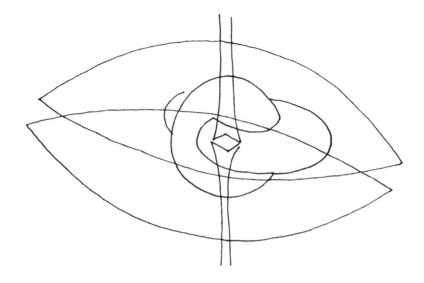

Example 6
The heart center of Jerusalem is very special. It is located under the Church of the Holy Sepulcher, which stands at the place of the destroyed Golgatha rock. The heart center can be contacted in the lowest crypt. It is basically composed of two double units, like the human heart. Two units are moving one around the other simultaneously in a vertical and horizontal direction. The other two units, looking shell-like, move rhythmically one into the other, in and out. These movements all are centered on a heart atom at the center.

Centers corresponding to the upper chakras

The correspondence between Earth energy centers and the chakra line along the human spine is not very obvious after we pass the fourth chakra. Differences between the human and landscape organisms become more apparent. However, it may be helpful to provide some glimpses.

Throat chakra
The breathing system of the landscape could be considered to correspond to the fifth human chakra. The throat chakra is associated with

the power to create. Symbolically we speak of the power of the Word. This aspect of the throat chakra is related to special chakras of the landscape that I call "creative centers." They are composed of different tubes emerging out of the Earth's depth. Each of the tubes represents a channel through which a different kind of Earth creative force is emanating. The chakra is composed in such a way that different creative qualities merge to produce a creative pool ("word") of energy. Often the interaction of the creative center with the larger cosmic holon is of decisive importance to its function. I believe the function of the creative centers is to further the Earth creative processes.

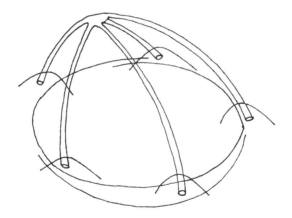

Example 1
I found one of the first examples of an Earth creative chakra at East Troy, not far from Chicago. The holon of the place is composed of a large field surrounded by five hills. Each hill represents a focus of one of the tubes of the chakra. The tubes form an etheric cupola above the landscape. Within the space of the cupola the intermingling of different creative powers takes place. From there creative powers are dispersed throughout the landscape. The cupola is complemented by a flat underground "dish" filled with something very precious, like archetypal patterns of creation.

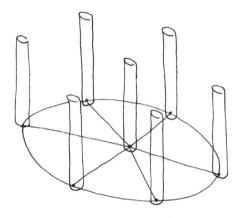

Example 2
This example comes from Almaty, Kazakhstan. The creative chakra located at the southern edge of the city is composed of six vertical pillars positioned in a circle around the seventh one. The whole composition is approximately 3000 meters in diameter. The pillars are interconnected to form a kind of wheel of life. The central pillar holds the proper energy balance for the whole composition. The six pillars surrounding the central pillar connect the cosmic creative force to six different aspects of the Earth's creative powers that are needed to make life possible on the material level. They can be called feminine/masculine interaction, fertility powers, wisdom, the Earth time rhythms, knowledge of creation, and the power of grounded love.

Chakra of the third eye
There are at least two kinds of Earth energy centers that correspond to the chakra of the third eye, centers that store Earth memory and centers of equilibrium. The first ones can be compared to the function of the brain, and the second ones can be compared to the two equilibrium organs positioned in our ears.

The center of Earth memory represents the storage of knowledge that helps to understand life processes on the Earth surface. The wisdom of the Earth is all-present in this center. Some of these places seem to store knowledge gathered by ancient civilizations that disappeared long ago. Traditionally places of oracles were located above such memory centers to provide wisdom needed for answering questions posed by pilgrims.

Since the Earth holon is composed of many different energy systems, dimensions, and evolutions, they must be held in equilibrium. For this purpose the Earth Soul has developed different balancing systems. The planetary equilibrium system is composed of an unknown number of gigantic light balls positioned in different landscapes around the globe. With the help of its axis, each of the light balls is anchored in the Earth core from where equilibrium is being maintained. To develop sensitivity regarding the condition on the Earth's surface, each equilibrium sphere is half-sunk into the Earth surface organism. With the help of two horizontal triangles the equilibrium sphere is connected to the given landscape.

Yet another equilibrium system has the task of balancing the energy fields of the planet. One of the main centers of this system is located in Venice, Italy. There are also local equilibrium organs, composed of a vertical light column and a light sphere balancing at its top.

Example 1
The drawing shows a center of Earth memory located behind a medieval church in Turnisce in the very east of Slovenia. A light pillar emerging out of the Earth opens into a large light sphere. Within the sphere there are drawer-like storages of memory. The church itself is also a treasure of memory, since the interior is covered with medieval fresco paintings. Similar memory centers are found on Churchill Square in Prague, Czech Republic, and in the midst of Sao Paulo, Brazil, between the park of Ibirapuera and Parque da Alimacao.

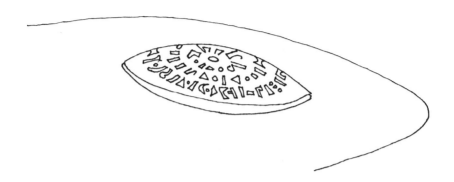

Example 2
Sometimes Earth memory centers show the form of an etheric disc "buried" horizontally under the ground. A center of this kind marks the place in Medjugorje, Bosnia, where the Virgin Mary has been appearing regularly since 1983. I was present at an appearance on September 15th, 2006. I could observe that the Earth Soul, identifying with the Mother of the universe, uses the capacity of that disc to appear in its etheric form to people. The disc is incised with hieroglyphs (information carriers) of an unknown kind.

Example 3
This example shows a typical local equilibrium organ that is composed of a vertical light column and a light sphere balancing at its top. I observed the one depicted here at Eberharting, Bavaria.

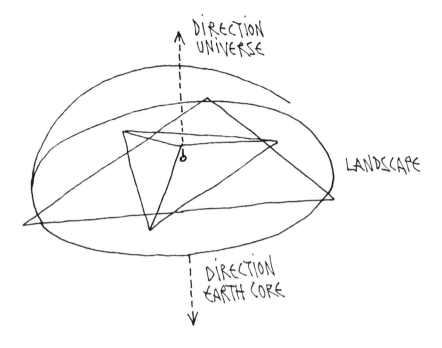

Example 4
The drawing shows one of the planetary equilibrium centers located at
Villach, Austria. It has a diameter of approximately 25 miles. The smaller
triangle forms a three-sided pyramid around the organ's axis. The larger
triangle anchors the chakra's holon in the surrounding landscape.

Crown chakra correspondences
The task of the crown chakra, located at the highest point of the human
body, is to hold upright the living connection between the human being
and the universe of spirit. Similarly the crown centers of a landscape
connect the microcosmos of the given landscape with the larger holon
of the universal whole. Places of the crown chakra can be recognized
by the overwhelming sensation that the Earth and cosmos are joined
in that location. The Earth-Cosmos relationship is based upon a two-
way communication. The qualities of the star world are descending
through the crown center deep down into the Earth. The impulses of
the Earth Soul are ascending toward Heaven.

Another kind of Earth chakra is complementary to the crown centers. They can be called "centers of connection between different levels of existence." They are not primarily oriented from the universe to the Earth core, but the opposite, from the Earth core upwards toward the cosmos. They enable communication between the Earth and cosmos to function in a different way than the crown centers. They perform the same task but in a more organic, feminine way, as opposed to crown centers, which can be very overpowering and masculine.

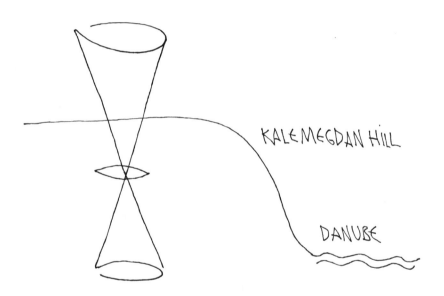

Example 1
The crown center of Belgrade, Serbia, is located upon a granite "head" called Kalemegdan, overlooking the confluence of two mighty rivers, the Sava and Danube. It can be found at the left side of the entrance to the large complex of Kalemegdan Fortress. The etheric form of the center looks like a sandglass. It appears as two conic spaces meeting with their cones inside the disc-like center, which is located underground. The two components of the sandglass form are opened respectively to the width of the universe and the core of the Earth.

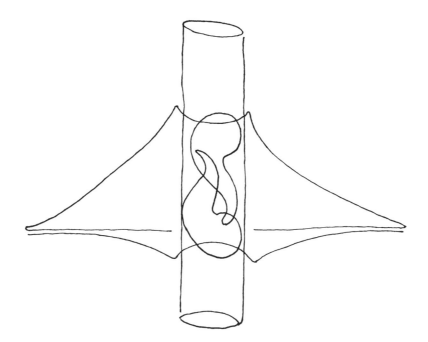

Example 2
The crown center of the Dead Sea area at Qumran, Israel, is more complex. It looks like a large golden tube reaching from the vastness of the universe toward the Earth core. Within the tube an organ of connection is moving rhythmically up and down. It looks like Heaven and Earth being sewn together. The center is located a bit higher above the ancient Essene settlement. At the level of the settlement the impulses of the Earth/Cosmos exchange form a disc-like energy field surrounding the tube, and extend into the landscape.

Example 3
This example shows a typical feminine kind of crown chakra, a cen-
ter of connection between different levels of existence. Within the two
large tubes are spaces located at different levels, like different stories in
a building. They represent portals to different dimensions of existence.
Different dimensions and levels of existence are described in the first two
parts of the present book.

3.3 Archetypal powers behind reality

The previous chapter was dedicated to different organs whose task it is to nourish life processes at the Earth surface. But to be able to nourish, the chakras of the Earth have to be nourished themselves! We have emphasized that the primary function of the Earth chakras (Earth vital-energy centers) is to transform "raw" primeval energy into life force that can be absorbed and digested by the landscape organism and the different beings inhabiting it. Now is the time to ask ourselves—what is this "raw" primeval energy, and how does it appear within our space of reality?

The nourishing system of the Earth

First of all, the basic nourishing system of the Earth tends to be hidden as much as possible, not just to our eyes, but also to inner perception. This hidden aspect may be a security precaution. The basis of life has to be protected. But there may also be a human factor involved: the fear of chaos, the fear of darkness, the fear of forces that cannot be controlled by mental consciousness. The human imagination uses different images to try to understand the nourishing system of the Earth even if its essence cannot be explained logically. The ancient Greeks spoke of the dark side of the cosmos, which they called "chaos." Out of the terrible disorder of chaos, the order of cosmos (the space of reality) appears.

Another image is that of dragons, an image that is found throughout Eastern and Western cultures. These terrible, merciless creatures abide either within the depths of the Earth or in the darkness of interstellar space. Their power is so potent that people die from interacting with the dragon, unless they are equipped with special divine gifts, like the so-called "dragon slayers." Our understanding of this image is that the slaying of the dragon means that the chaotic archetypal powers of the Earth and cosmos can be transmuted into life-nourishing energies if they undergo a certain transformation. For a given landscape, its vital-energy system works as a transformer.

In a modern context human beings experience the dragon power in a very real, immediate, and physical manner through the power of nuclear energy. Recall the terrible images of Hiroshima and Nagasaki, or the awesome mushroom clouds of atomic bomb tests in deserted locations! Consider the disaster of Chernobyl and the ticking time bombs of spent fuel from nuclear energy power plants. The Greek idea of chaos applies directly to the attempts of scientific culture to develop the means of controlling atomic power—woe if it gets out of our programed order! Then the ancient dragon shows its deadly might.

Mythology tells us about earthly as well as atmospheric dragons. The Greeks imagined the cosmos as surrounded by chaos. One meaning of this image is that we should not press the dragon power down into the subconsciousness of the Earth. We are surrounded by "dragon power" and carry it within ourselves as the power of our atoms.

The atomic power of the dragon represents the basic power of creation. It manifests as *"the nourishing system of the Earth"* to nourish the vital-energy organs of the landscape, so that they in turn can nourish all the different life forms of the Earth surface.

Within the holon of the human being the nourishing system can be identified with our back space and with the chakras of the back. The light side of the body, the front side, together with its chakra systems is engaged in daily creativity. The power needed for that creativity is conveyed through several horizontal light channels from the reservoir of the back chakras to the front chakras as needed.

Knots of archetypal powers

There are different ways through which the existence of the nourishing system of the Earth can be detected in a landscape. One possibility is to tune to phenomena that I would like to call *"knots of archetypal powers."* They appear as clusters of phenomena wrapped inside the etheric underground or atmospheric tissue of a given place. At one time I called them "sources of archetypal powers." However, I later discovered that the term "source" is not appropriate, since nothing is flowing out of those "knots."

These knots simply seem to hold their primeval chaotic power within themselves. Their function could be compared to battery chargers. They seem to serve as potentials for living beings, environmental spirits and life processes to be recharged with the primeval potential of life so that their life systems can work properly.

The surprising characteristic of these knots is that they do not show any constant characteristics. Their spinning dynamics may be related to the deep underground, while at the same time they relate to the star movements of the sky. They may simultaneously show feminine and masculine qualities, even if they seem to be neutral. The knots of archetypal powers are capable of appearing in different forms. One time they may appear to be located deep within the underground, while at another time they may spin in the atmosphere above a place.

Clusters of chaotic knots may not be useful for the geomantic mapping of a given place, but how fortunate that they exist within a given holon! In this time of planetary transformation they are becoming an important factor of change. While tuning into one of these knots their transformative power can be experienced in one's body as a kind of revitalizing shower. (See Chapter 3.8.)

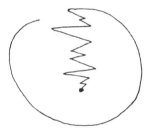

Example 1
The knot of primeval powers is located underground. At the same time its presence stays in resonance with the cosmic whole.

Example 2
In the depths of the Earth I see a fast milling wheel. One aspect of its force is concentrating, while the other is pushing outwardly.

Example 3
The power of the knot extends underground in the shape of a T (or tau-cross). At the same time it is spinning above the ground, very concentrated and fast. The body sensation is like many tiny explosions occurring everywhere within the body tissue.

Paths of the dragon

The atomic power of the nourishing system does not belong to the Earth surface. It provokes death and destruction if it is pulled into the manifested level of life. However, the European tradition of geomancy indicates a secret way through which the "dragon powers" touch the manifested level of life. It refers to so-called "dragon trails," paths along which "dragons move secretly across the landscape." They leave behind them a trail of life-nourishing powers, which can be absorbed by living beings of the related environment, including humans.

Translated into logical language, this image implies that the immediate presence of atomic power, the foundation of life force, would be too destructive if encountered directly. But providing an etheric imprint "at the back side of the Earth surface" becomes a means of accessing this power. This imprint can be perceived as an organically shaped stream of fiery energy, much like an invisible stream of volcanic lava, remaining close to the ground and floating along with a slow, majestic rhythm.

We can also understand "dragon paths" as streams of sexual forces of nature which fertilize all aspects of her kingdom. In pre-Christian times pilgrim paths were often located along these lines of the Earth's sexual force to celebrate Gaia's creative powers. This tradition was followed into the early Middle Ages when churches were frequently sited along these "dragon paths" to ensure a proper balance between the sexual powers of the Earth and the spiritual powers of the universe.

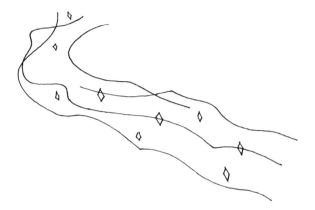

Example 1
The power stream of a "dragon path" floats partly above but mostly below the Earth surface. It is composed of earth and fire ethers.

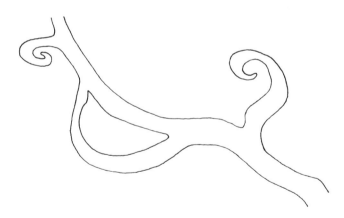

Example 2
The flow form of a "dragon path" is organic, like river streams. Often tributary streams branch off from the main dragon path to touch upon some important geomantic features located in the surrounding landscape. The "branches" either end in a spiral or they join the main stream later.

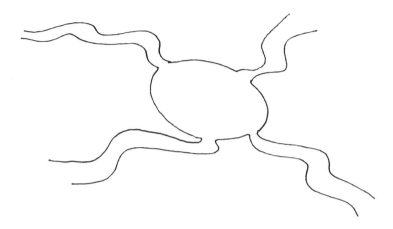

Example 3
*Major Earth chakras tend to be sources of "dragon path" streams. At
the edge of the chakra body one can sense several streams of the archetypal powers of the Earth moving in different directions.*

The power system of mountains and oceans

Salty oceans and ranges of high mountains are distributed all over the
surface of the Earth. Imagine the number of majestic mountain peaks,
like those in the Himalayas, Rocky Mountains, Andes, or Alps! Imagine the vast and incredibly deep oceans! Mountains and oceans are both
associated with the power of crystals. Salt and minerals are crystalline
in structure and are capable of absorbing and storing immense quanti-
ties of cosmic powers entering the Earth holon.

At the same time oceans and mountains are permeated by the archetypal powers of Gea from inside the Earth. An alchemical process is
continuously underway within mountains and oceans through which
the powers of the nourishing system of the Earth, the deadly "dragon
powers," are transmuted into life-giving energies. The interaction with
the cosmic forces absorbed by the crystalline substance of oceans and
mountains enables this process to take place. The interaction of the
archetypal powers of the Earth and cosmos brings into being, deep
within oceans and mountains, a well-balanced power carrying the quality of love capable of reconciling opposites. This interaction serves to
further life processes rather than sow destruction or death.

The immense weight of mountains and oceans presses the transmuted archetypal powers of mountain ranges and oceans through subterranean channels in the Earth toward lowlands, where they appear as etheric sources. The principle of their distribution resembles that of artesian wells. The heart powers of mountains and oceans, pushed through underground channels, appear as etheric sources scattered throughout lowlands.

These underground channels can be detected through dowsing techniques. They are often mistaken as underground water streams. To distinguish them from ordinary channels of underground water, they are called "sacred water lines"—even if they do not carry any water. The power system of mountains and oceans can be compared with our gland system. The chemistry of the gland system of the human body works to translate chakra impulses into the physical level. The power system of mountains and oceans works to translate the over-powerful archetypal forces of the Earth and cosmos into life-sustaining powers.

Further, the result of the alchemy that takes place within mountains and oceans is a power of the heart, an all-loving power that can be understood as pure love emanating from the intercourse between the virgin Earth and the father Heaven.

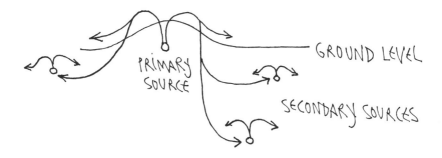

Example 1
This example illustrates the principle by which the sources of mountains and oceans are distributed throughout the landscape. Each main source is underground, feeding bunches of smaller sources.

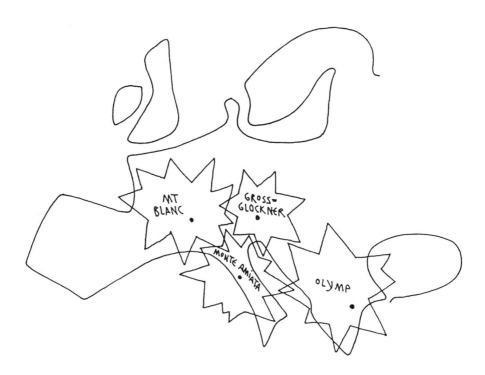

Example 2
This example shows the map of Europe with some of its most distinguished sacred mountains. The star-like forms reflect how far their sources extend.

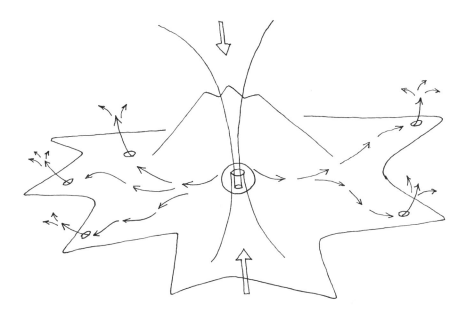

Example 3
This example shows a sketch of one of the holy mountains of Europe, the highest mountain of Austria, Grossglockner. Within the spherical center, the heart of the mountain, an alchemical process is taking place. We see the foot of the mountain that extends 200 miles. Also depicted are the underground distribution of transmuted energies and the appearance of singular sources in the lowlands.

3.4 Channels of vital power

After an intermezzo with the nourishing system of the Earth, we return to the vital-energy systems in the landscape. We devoted some attention to the archetypal powers that represent the foundation of all life-sustaining systems on the Earth surface. But now we will consider the third etheric system of the landscape.

We previously described vital-energy fields and centers of vital power (the Earth chakras). Now we will turn to so-called "linear phenomena" in the landscape.

The centers of vital power have a relatively fixed position within the landscape structure. But let's now consider "transport systems." In the landscape we find not only fixed structures like trees, mountains, valleys, houses, and cities—we also find dynamic elements like floating rivers, animal paths, roads, airline routes, electric circuits, and highways. We intend to approach this kind of phenomena under the term "channels of vital powers."

We are not considering the physical level of transportation, but its etheric counterpart. We will address energy lines, ley-lines, energy paths, and dragon lines, including etheric channels that cross a given landscape on different levels and in different directions, following different purposes.

In our previous discussion of Earth energy centers we stated that our chakra system can serve as a means of orientation and understanding regarding the different roles of vital-energy centers. This approach also can be partly applied in the case of linear phenomena in the landscape, but the comparison with different chakras is not relevant in this case.

Here we can refer only to different levels characterized by particular chakras. In effect we are speaking of different energy channels linking chakras, or of channels transporting basic life powers to different chakra systems.

When we described the different vital-energy centers of the Earth surface we started with the basic chakras and moved upwards. This time let's start in the opposite direction, with the highest level, with the channels of cosmic power.

Cosmic power channels

The channels of cosmic power refer to the level of the three upper chakras. They cross the landscape in different directions, high in the atmosphere, like planes flying intercontinental flights. Through the means of resonance they leave distinct traces on the ground. Together they form a network of light channels that surround and embrace the Earth. By sensing their resonance on the Earth, it is possible to experience the location and specific qualities of a given channel of cosmic force. The trace on the ground is about 40 meters wide.

Channels of cosmic power can be considered as the opposite pole of the "dragon paths" described previously. The dragon paths transport the sexual force of the Earth while the cosmic channels transport information concerning the spiritual aspects of creation. They distribute the archetypal knowledge needed for the creation of any aspect of life to manifest throughout the Earth Cosmos. Without the archetypal keys (archetypal information) held by the channels of cosmic power, the creative ideas of cosmos would remain floating ideas. They could not manifest in their etheric body, a precondition for incarnating later on the physical level.

The resonance path that can be felt on the ground under a cosmic channel transmits archetypal information carried by that channel of cosmic power to creative agents on the ground. The transmission works on the base of resonance. In summary, channels of cosmic power carry throughout the globe archetypal information needed to guide creative processes on the Earth surface in their proper direction.

Channels of life force (ley-lines)

How do we refer to phenomena that our everyday rational language excludes? Let's first try to describe the phenomena, and then find a term that might approximately fit.

The term "ley" is an ancient English word meaning "an old straight path." Alfred Watkins used this term in his 1925 book (*The Old Straight Path*) to give a name to straight geomantic lines that he discovered in some English landscapes. From the point of view of current geomancy, he was referring to "ley-lines" as alignments between historical sites,

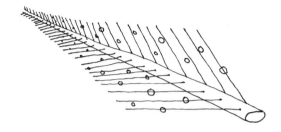

Example 1
I will try to describe a channel of cosmic power observed above the Adriatic Sea. The channel is composed of a core tube and a carrier structure positioned on both sides of the tube. The whole structure looks like a fish bone. The archetypal information is stored within the core tube. It is transmitted through innumerable light balls jumping from one extension of the "fish bone" to another.

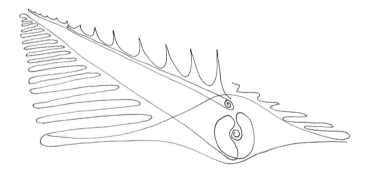

Example 2
Here I show a cross section of a channel of cosmic power observed above the Meissner mountain close to Kassel, Germany. The core tube of the channel is dual in its structure. The smaller tube above is enormously bright. It is responsible for connecting the cosmic channel with its spiritual purpose. The lower part of the tube shows a triple division. Central to it is a stream of cosmic archetypal power. The left side of the tube is reserved for transporting archetypal ideas of creation; the right side is for the patterns that make manifestation of life forms possible. At each side of the core tube one can perceive carrier structures that resemble a continuous series of bird wings.

which belong to the cultural layer of the landscape, but not to its natural organism.

Since that time the term "ley-line" has begun to be used in a different way. In the book *Ley-Lines and Ecology* (1983) William Bloom and I used this term to denote channels of life force that we perceive in the landscape as part of its life-sustaining etheric organism. We refer to ley-lines as energy paths distributing life force (prana) throughout the etheric organism of a landscape, similar to the way in which acupuncture meridians distribute life force within the human organism. To distinguish these channels of life force from Watkins' use of the term, I called them "power-leys."

Seen in my inner vision, a power ley-line appears as a dynamic composition of spiraling life force, piercing through the ambience of a given landscape in a straight but slightly undulating line. Imagine a fiery snake rolling through the landscape in great majesty, coiling uphill up and down, always following a straight path, which may cover a distance of many thousand miles. The following characteristics of power-leys may be helpful in identifying them:

- They vary in length from six miles up to thousands of miles. The short ones can be called "local leys," and the long ones "planetary leys."

- They follow a straight line while "moving" through the landscape and aligning to its relief. However, their course is not perfectly straight. They are undulating, and at certain points they are capable of slightly changing direction.

- They undulate above the Earth surface, partly underground, and vary in their width from four to eight meters.

- Power ley-lines are composed of etheric power vortices that are linked in chains to form a solid line. At the core of the vortex structure there is a narrow stream of archetypal Earth power, which represents the source of their power.

The chains of vortices anchor the power ley-line in the etheric field along its path. They also transform the archetypal powers of the ley's core into life force. The third aspect of their function is to absorb depleted etheric powers from the environment and renew them by bringing them into contact with the archetypal power within the core of the ley-lines. The chain of vortices then launches the renewed energies back into the etheric field of the given landscape.

Please understand that power ley-lines are not moving through the landscape like an express train—rather, they are standing! The vortex structure is moving with great speed while the line as a whole is standing still, performing its service to the landscape. And yet there is a sense of movement from the source of a given ley line toward its point of eventual disappearance. The source of a power ley is a place of profound importance. It is there that the basic power of a given ley-line is ushering out of the archetypal layer of the Earth. Its source provides a given ley with its unique characteristics.

This means that power ley-lines are individual phenomena. Each carries within its structure an individual code by which it can be recognized anywhere upon the Earth surface. It may be a geometrical code or a specific color combination. In a way they also take part in the consciousness dimension of a landscape. Superseding their vortex structure is a channel for transporting information. There is specific information that leys transport and distribute—the will of Gea to manifest life through matter.

Equilibrium leys

Referring to the vertical line of chakras in the human body, the cosmic power lines correspond to the level of the third eye, and power leys correspond to the throat level. They both perform the role of creators in the landscape.

Equilibrium leys correspond to the level of the heart chakra. Like the heart chakra, which balances the so called "upper" and "lower" chakras, equilibrium lines help to hold the balance of energies within places and landscapes. They complement the activity of the previously mentioned etheric equilibrium organs. The task of equilibrium leys is not to carry energy or information, but to balance energy fields. For this purpose they are polarized as Yin and Yang leys. By balancing their own polarities, they are capable of holding balance in the landscape.

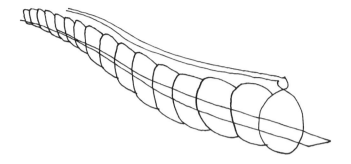

Example 1
This example shows a cross section through a power-ley that I have observed at Poultney, Vermont, USA. Leys always appear packed in protective etheric sheets. The core, carrying archetypal force (similar to a snake's tongue), and the vortex structure are both located within the main tube. Above it is a channel dedicated to the flow of information.

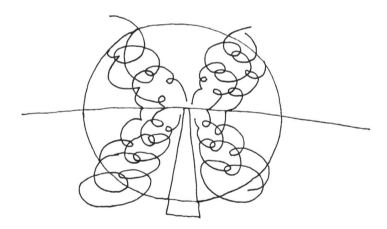

Example 2
This example shows a cross section of a power ley, as if one is standing inside of it, looking toward the horizon. The emphasis is upon the relationship between the vortex chains and the central vein of the archetypal force within the tube of a ley-line.

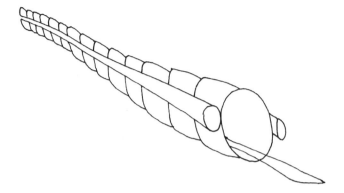

Example 3
This example shows the unusual structure of the power-ley pulsating between Würzburg, Germany, and Salzburg, Austria. At its left is a supplementary line giving stability to the ley structure, and the information channel is at its right. At the center is the strip of archetypal powers surrounded by a vortex structure.

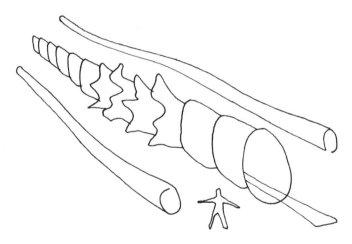

Example 4
This example shows a power ley observed at Kassel, Germany. The central ley structure has two "baby-leys" at the sides to secure the minimal functioning of a ley that has been heavily damaged through the absence of sensitivity by the present civilization. The human figure is there to give a sense of proportion.

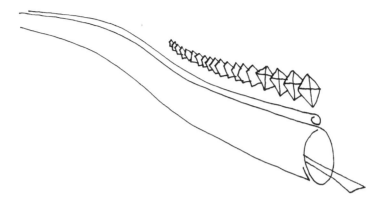

Example 5
This example shows the individual code of a ley observed close to Coburg, Bavaria, in Germany. The code pulsating along the line slightly above its structure shows the geometric form and color of a cut ruby with a cross inside.

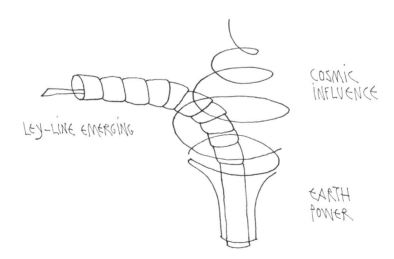

Example 6
This example shows the source of a ley-line in Oslo, Norway, which heads to Ljubljana, Slovenia. The source unites the "sexual intercourse" between Earth and Heaven with the moment of the ley-line's birth.

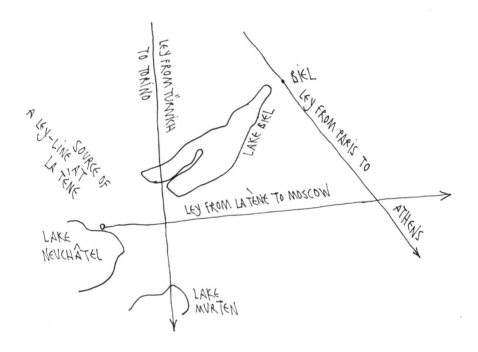

Labels in figure:
- TO TORINO
- LEY FROM TÜNNIKH
- A LEY-LINE SOURCE OF AT LA TÈNE
- LAKE BIEL
- BIEL
- LEY FROM PARIS TO
- ATHENS
- LEY FROM LA TÈNE TO MOSCOW
- LAKE NEUCHÂTEL
- LAKE MURTEN

Example 7
This example shows the usual density and distribution of planetary ley-lines in a landscape holon. It is the holon of Lake Biel, in Switzerland, with a diameter of approximately 20 miles.

Usually there are two straight equilibrium leys to be found within a holon, a Yin and a Yang. To accentuate the sense of balance within the given holon they usually cross each other at a certain point. There are cases when only one equilibrium ley pulsates within a landscape holon. Its sides are polarized according to the Yin-Yang principle. Polarized in this way, the ley extends into the landscape to balance it.

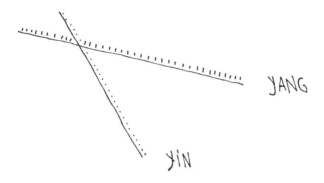

Example 1
Two polarized equilibrium leys cross each other.

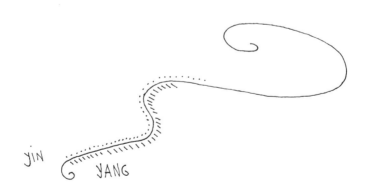

Example 2
A single polarized equilibrium ley as it winds in the Aare River valley east of Lake Murten, Switzerland.

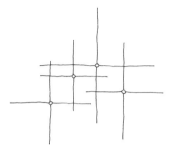

Example 3
In cases where the equilibrium is truly endangered, like in big cities, the Earth organism tends to manifest a peculiar equilibrium system of crossing lines approximately one mile long. Each arm vibrates in tune with one of the four elements. This example was observed in Ljubljana.

Watery (Yin) channels

As stated above, comparing our human chakra levels to linear phenomena at the Earth surface can provide a key for understanding the latter. Since the solar plexus chakra is responsible for our emotional powers, watery (Yin) channels can be attributed to the solar plexus level. It is the purpose of watery (Yin) channels to nourish the emotional fields of the landscape. They are closely connected to Gea, the Earth Soul, and are associated with the lunar cycle. In this sense the watery ley-channels represent an opposite to the power leys, which have a fiery character and pulsate with a solar rhythm. Watery ley-channels do not show distinct forms as do power leys. Rather they can be perceived as streams within the emotional energy field of a place or landscape floating slightly above the Earth surface. They are powerful in a feminine way. It is the quality of the watery ley-channels that is important, not their structure. They carry certain emotional qualities across the Earth surface and distribute them throughout places and landscapes. The qualities of watery leys have an energetic character and posses their own power, like our emotions.

Watery (Yin) channels are often associated with rivers, lakes, seas and oceans, even if they are not identical with the etheric body of these water bodies. They are relatives of rivers and oceanic streams, pulsating at the etheric level. They tend to have their sources within the water chakras of oceans or lakes and carry the corresponding qualities to and throughout the surrounding material landscape.

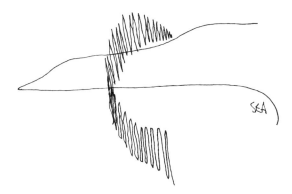

Example 1
This example shows a watery channel appearing out of a large sea chakra south of Carnac, France, carrying the quality of the ocean across the peninsula of Brittany, and disappearing in the Atlantic Ocean after it has crossed the western tip of Cornwall, England.

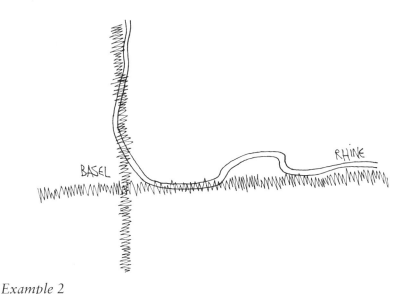

Example 2
The Rhine River makes a 90-degree turn at Basel. From Lake Constance it flows eastward toward Basel. There the Rhine makes a sharp turn to continue its flow in a northern direction toward Cologne. In each direction the Rhine is followed by a watery ley-channel. They cross at Basel and continue to flow in their westward and southward directions.

Acceleration channels

If you are looking for a correspondence between the level of the sexual chakra and linear phenomena in the landscape, please refer to the chapter on dragon paths. Dragon paths belong to those geomantic phenomena that can be located in more than one chapter. But if we consider dragon paths as linear phenomena of the landscape, they correspond to the second chakra level.

However, there are linear geomantic phenomena that do not correspond to chakra levels. Some of them will be addressed in regard to the manifested forms of landscape (Chapter 3.6, Animal track lines and aquastats). But I would like to mention two of them here.

Acceleration channels

The human etheric structure has acceleration channels connecting singular units of its chakra system. The most well known is the acceleration channel along the backbone that connects the seven vertical chakras. There are also horizontal channels, for example those connecting different chakras of the heart system. Something like this can also occur within the landscape. If the Gea-consciousness would like to strengthen certain aspects of the etheric organism, the relevant vital-energy center can be replicated or multiplied, and singular subcenters then connected through an acceleration channel. This happens often during the present period of Earth changes. I have discovered that most often heart centers are being strengthened in this way. I call such channels "acceleration channels" because they work as accelerators of the power centers they connect.

Acupuncture system

Within the organism of the human body the acupuncture system is composed of tiny channels carrying life force throughout the organism. This function is performed in the landscape by power-leys. The acupuncture system of the landscape has a different function. As an information transport system it is composed of fine underground threads resembling human nerves that form a network. The network is organic in its form, composed of impulses of air ethers. The threads of the "nerves" are so fine that hardly they can be felt.

What is important and can be detected on the Earth surface are sensors positioned along acupuncture lines certain distances from each other. They serve as collectors of information needed by Gea and her

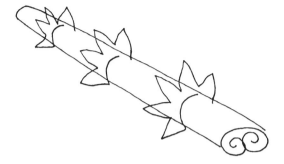

Example 1
Ancient cultures were capable of building artificial acceleration chan-
nels. For this purpose they erected straight rows of stones (the most
well-known are those from Carnac, France) or snake-like earth works.
While pilgrims were walking along or upon those structures their energy
systems were accelerated and they were brought into a trance state to
experience deeper dimensions of reality. This example is from Chosen
Hill, Tewkesbury, England. The flame structures refer to the transform-
ing presence of fire spirits.

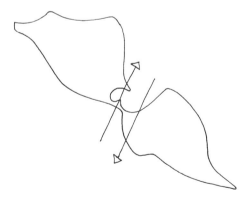

Example 2
This example shows a pair of acceleration channels that I discovered
during lithopuncture work in Quito, Ecuador. They serve to help bal-
ance the energy fields of the Atlantic and Pacific Oceans.

consciousness units to properly react to situations upon the Earth surface. Sensors can be identified as acupuncture points of the given landscape. They look like two conic vessels rubbing against each other with their edges. Sound information produced in this way can be "heard" in the depth of the Earth.

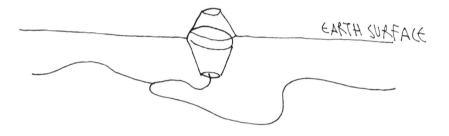

Example
This example show how one can imagine a sensor belonging to the acupuncture system of the Earth.

3.5 Elemental consciousness

We now come to a critical moment in the development of this part of *Sacred Geography*. We must now shift our attention from energy to consciousness, and from consciousness to the living presence of beings. Can we speak about the geomantic phenomena of places and landscapes without considering conscious beings?

So we will change gears. The central consideration regarding vital-energy centers, the etheric form, becomes secondary. We now move to the primary role that single beings play within the landscape holon.

It is important to understand that in dealing with the elemental world, nature, and environmental spirits, we do not mean that we encounter individualized beings like humans. Such an understanding of the elemental world is basically incorrect. Perceiving a consciousness dimension within a given landscape in the form of elemental beings means to perceive holographic units of one single consciousness, the consciousness of Gea, the Earth Soul. As holographic units of the all-embracing Gea-consciousness, even if we do encounter elemental beings as individual light-and-consciousness phenomena in the landscape, from their point of view they are always an indivisible part of the whole.

We can speak of different levels of Gea-consciousness. The archetypal consciousness concentrated within the inner layers of the Earth holds the treasury of Gea wisdom inside the Earth. Beings of the elemental world represent that particular aspect of Earth consciousness that is reaching out toward the disc-like membrane of the Earth surface to guide life processes manifested within its multidimensional space.

The role of elemental beings is to dive again and again deep "down" into the soul consciousness of the Earth (Gea). From there they bring to the Earth surface impulses that are directing and modeling all the different life processes on the physical level. To perform this multifaceted task their evolution has brought forth all the variations of elemental beings and nature spirits needed to deal with each and every single life form, from vast landscapes to the tiny sand corn.

Get to know elemental world

Elemental beings have a double body in order to mediate between the soul consciousness of the Earth and the manifested life forms like plants, animals, mountain ranges, weather storms and human beings. On one side they are pure consciousness, able to merge with the Earth Soul and take part in her knowledge of creation. On the other they must have an etheric body able to approach materialized life forms and cooperate practically with them.

To cooperate practically with manifested life forms like mountain ranges, storms, human beings, and animals, elemental beings:

- guide the life-giving powers that permeate manifested forms of life,
- hold the intensity of those powers at a certain level,
- establish the appropriate quality of the given power, and
- coordinate different energy impulses or processes within a given holon.

To master this enormous task, relating to all the different levels of existence, the elemental consciousness has established its own evolutionary scale. Each elemental being, as an atom of Gea's soul, is moving along three basic levels of the elemental evolution.

1. Elemental beings that belong to the first evolutionary level are capable of performing one simple task, for example accompanying the growth of a single tree.

2. Those belonging to the second level are more highly evolved elemental beings responsible for guiding complex processes, like monitoring the cycles of nature and their influence on the whole variety of different living beings within a given holon.

3. Elemental beings belonging to the third evolutionary level can be referred to as Earth angels. For example, their task is to connect a landscape unit with the Earth's Soul purpose for that particular place. They belong to the sacred dimension of landscape.

Following this triple order of development, each unit of Gea-consciousness begins with performing simple tasks upon the Earth surface (step 1). Moving forward upon this evolutionary scale means to take responsibility for complex life processes. We speak of more highly evolved elemental beings and nature spirits (step 2). Finally they reach the highest step of their evolution, called master elemental consciousness (step 3). After that their evolution turns upside down. They become part of the archetypal core of the Earth Soul, which can be compared with the state of nirvana.

Exercise 1
A possible way to perceive elemental beings is to show yourself as part of their world, as people of the ancient cultures always did. Imagine yourself "decorated" with plants and leaves, with colors upon your face ... Then quickly detach yourself from your imagination and open to what you perceive.

Exercise 2
When you find a place where an elemental being is focused, remain there for a while, peacefully centered within your heart chakra. When you are ready, open yourself to the elemental being without any expectations or preconceptions. Stay present in your heart and, at the same time, listen to your surroundings and feel into the atmosphere or ambience. Do not start to explore on your own. Wait patiently for the being to reveal itself to you in its own way.

Exercise 3
One of the chakras for perceiving elemental beings and nature spirits is the solar plexus chakra in its emotional aspect. This aspect is focused some inches away from your physical body, within your aura and in front of your solar plexus, as a secondary solar plexus chakra. Imagine reaching from there in an emotionally sensitive way toward the place where you are sensing the elemental being to be. Imagine using an appendage or sensor like insects do, reaching out from the secondary chakra.

Exercise 4
Offer an exchange with elemental beings that you have perceived. Imagine taking your head into your hands, as if it were a light ball. Give it (make the proper gesture with your hands!) to the elemental beings present, to be held by them for a few moments while you are, in exchange, receiving insights about them. Put your "head" back in its place, and give thanks. This is an exercise designed to avoid the all-pervasive control that our minds try to exert.

Exercise 5
Imagine a golden ball jumping ceremoniously within the area of your waist. At a decisive moment lift the ball up to your heart space, open it, and perceive.

Beings of the four elements

The second principle that the evolution of elemental beings and environmental spirits follows is a division according to the four elements concept. Each unit of Gea-consciousness working at the Earth's surface belongs either to the elements of water, fire, earth or air. Currently there are also beings that do not follow this kind of division (described in the next chapter).

Element Water
Beings related to the water element first of all represent the consciousness permeating rivers, lakes, oceanic waves, water drops, and so forth. Traditionally they are called nixes and undines. More evolved nixes serve along the shores of lakes, streams, and rivers. Their task is to distribute the life-sustaining qualities of water throughout the surrounding landscape. They perform their task through resonance triggered by their dance-like movements. Nymphs guarding water sources belong to more highly evolved water beings. They embody the identity of streams, diverse rivers, marshes, and so on. Traditionally they were known as river Goddesses or Gods. They appear also as Devas representing the identity of watery landscapes.

Exercise
To perceive water beings one can use the language of traditional symbols attributed to them. Standing in front of a water body, imagine that your buttocks are covered with fish scales and your legs are shaped like a movable fish tail. Then quickly detach yourself from your imagination and open yourself instantly to perception.

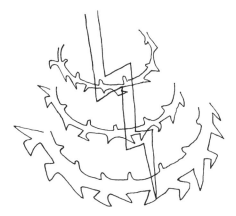

Example 1
This example shows nixes dancing around a lightning flash representing a focus of cosmic power inside the canyon of the River Aare at Meiringen, Switzerland, and distributing its quality throughout the landscape.

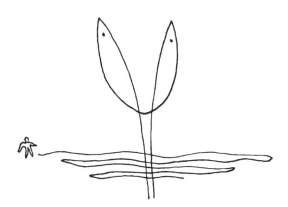

Example 2
This example shows a nymph of the river Vltava that I contacted in Prague after the great flood in 2005. She expressed her happiness at being able to reach into the city structure again, through the flood event, after the city had built up walls to protect its safety against flooding. The human figure is depicted to provide a sense of proportion.

Element Fire
The beings of the fire element supervise the processes of change, transformation, death, and transmutation. First of all they work to decompose all kinds of material forms when their purpose is finished, and to guide the powers "frozen" in form back to the original ocean of vibration. In this sense the elemental beings of fire consider themselves to be harbingers of freedom, guiding manifested forms back to the state of pure light. This leads the spirits of fire to the next step of their evolution to embody light, which means providing a consciousness body for light qualities within the manifested world. This step concerns the transformative qualities of light, the light of the soul, and the spiritual aspects of light. This process eventually brings them, related to the third step of their evolution, to become light messengers, carriers of ideas and inspirations. The ancient Greeks knew them as the Muses. Today they may be working in the transmission of inspired texts that sensitive persons receive from the spiritual world.

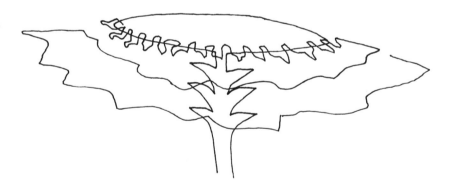

Example 1
This drawing shows a center of fire spirits at Schwarzenberger Park, Vienna, Austria, next to a pompous Soviet monument celebrating a Russian victory in World War II. The center looks like a fire geyser opening like a flower. The edges of "the flower" are bordered with fire spirits and their activity is widely distributed throughout the city in waves.

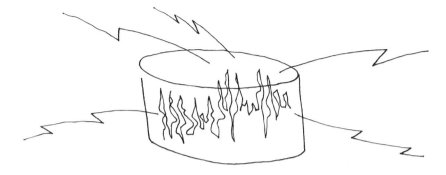

Example 2
This example shows a center of fire spirits at the edge of a marshy lake at the Spirit Fire Retreat Center, Leyden, Massachusetts. The fire beings dance continuously within a closed area that serves as resonance space for their activity in the landscape.

Exercise
To get a good perception of fire beings, one should concentrate on the warmth and pulsation of the blood within one's own veins—which represents the fire element within our body. Open your perception from there.

Element Earth
The beings of the Earth element are basically working with the process of energy manifestation and the materialization of forms. If we take on one hand the distinct forms of a landscape, a plant, or a rock, and on the other the blueprint or archetypal pattern behind their existence, the beings of the Earth element represent the bridge between the two extremes. Imagine the universe full of different vibrations, full of primeval light. The consciousness that we associate with the Earth element is constantly weaving from light vibrations those units that, when combined, lead to the emergence of forms. But this weaving of the manifested body of reality cannot be done just once—even if it

looks that way to our materialistic point of view. The tapestry of manifested reality must be woven constantly in order to continue to exist in a given moment.

Earth element beings perform the gigantic task of holding the world in its forms while taking part at the basic level of their evolution. The Western tradition usually calls them "dwarfs." The consciousness of the advanced level of this evolution involves innumerable efforts in manifesting different forms of reality, coordinating them so that a harmonious world composition emerges in each moment. This concerns not only the world in its entirety but also the micro-universe of each holon, be it the holon of a tiny plant, of a human body, or of a large landscape. I usually call the corresponding being or consciousness function Pan, the Greek name for the God of Nature. By Pan I mean the guiding intelligence of the Earth element consciousness performing its service within a given landscape holon. Using the God of Nature's name for this purpose lends these advanced beings a touch or recognition of divinity, which they deserve. Another role or being of the advanced level is the "old sage," who concentrates the wisdom and knowledge related to a given place.

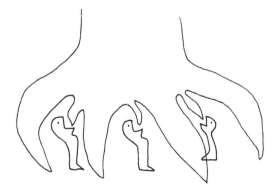

Example 1
During a workshop on elemental beings that I held at the Omega Institute at Rhinebeck, NY, USA, a tall tree showed me how it collects information from the surrounding landscape holon and sends it through its roots to the earth elementals as a kind of a feedback on their creation.

Example 2
During a workshop held at Hawkwood College, Stroud, England, a tall dwarf appeared to me underground. To explain the role that he and his kind perform in nature, he let flowers grow out of his consciousness. A complete landscape grew in front of me, with animals jumping around ...

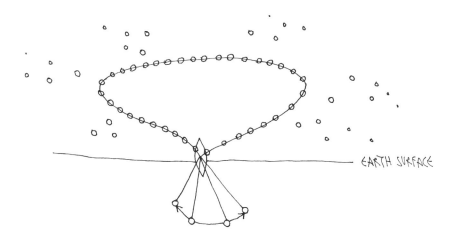

Example 3
This example shows a Pan focus observed at Leyden, Massachusetts, USA. The core of Pan's presence is focussed at the ground level. To perform its functions, the Pan presence showed me two of his extensions. The underground aspect looks like a swinging pendulum that is measuring and directing time cycles of nature. The atmospheric aspect looks like a collection of little balls containing information. Balls are flying constantly out to different corners of "his" holon and returning with information needed to conduct the process of manifestation properly.

Example 4
This shows a Pan focus observed at Strawberry Fields, Central Park, New York. The Pan-consciousness presented itself as a large sphere capable of mirroring all life forms existing within its holon. The needed corrective information was mirrored back to single units of the manifested world.

Exercise
To perceive the earth elemental beings, imagine that you have roots spreading underground. At the tip of each root, you have an eye. Look around simultaneously with several of those eyes.

Element Air
Beings belonging to the air element deal with all the different kinds of interactions and processes that go on in a given ambience. Usually we refer to these interactions as the world of fairies. At the basic level of their evolution, groups of fairies act as conductors in front of an orchestra. There are billions of life processes moving within a given holon, like a multitude of tones produced by different instruments. The fairy consciousness is responsible for harmonizing them all—not only working on harmony between all the moving processes, but also harmonizing them with the cosmic cycles and the outgoing impulses of the Earth Soul.

But please understand that elemental beings do not "work." According to fairy tales they only play and dance. Translated into logical language, they are constantly performing rituals through which their influence upon energy and matter is manifested. More advanced beings of the air element are known as Devas, keepers of archetypes.

The plant Devas embody blueprints of plant species to guide the building of single plants, a "work" done by the Earth element beings. Devas of landscapes embody the unique identity of different landscapes as information needed by all aspects of consciousness creating within a given landscape.

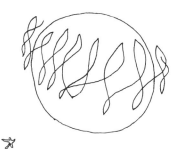

Example 1
This example shows a center of fairies observed in the atmosphere of Francke Park in Berlin, Germany. The center is composed of a light sphere imbued with information. A circle of fairies is constantly dancing around according to a specific rhythm, performing their ritual work. A human figure is drawn to give a sense of proportion.

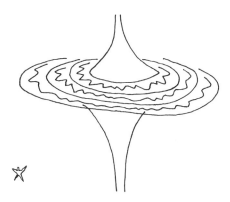

Example 2
To emphasize the enormous variability of fairy centers, I chose this example of another air element center from Berlin, this one from Tempelhof. It looks like a spinning top. Fairies in rows are "dancing" around a double funnel, providing information from the Earth and cosmos.

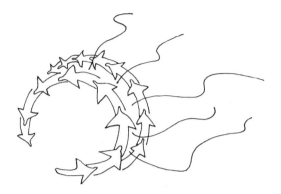

Example 3
This example shows a fairy center observed at a park in Udine, Italy. The center is composed of two rows of "dancing" fairies parallel to each other. During different phases of the ritual dance the two rows move apart to provide space for information to be transmitted.

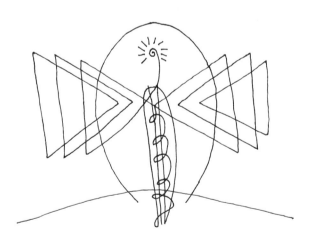

Example 4
This example shows the landscape Deva of the Dreznica high plateau, over Soca Valley, Slovenia. What appears like wings moving constantly is the means by which communication with the corresponding landscape is made possible. The Deva appears as tall as a church belfry.

Exercise

To experience the fairy presence in the atmosphere of a holon, imagine that you have double wings like a flying horse—transparent and long-shaped wings. Imagine lifting yourself high into the air. There you are, moving your wings through the power of your heart. Then suddenly become still, remain in the air, and perceive without hesitation. When you feel that you may loose height, activate your wings again for a while, and continue your exploration. Finally descend back to Earth and ground yourself again.

Consciousness of the fifth element — ethers

Since 1998 it has been possible to perceive a new generation of elemental beings and nature spirits. These beings of consciousness cannot be associated with any of the four elements, whereby they have been named the fifth Element. This Element comprises all of the other Four Elements in their etheric form. Let us list some of their characteristics:

- The new generation of environmental spirits is not bound to a specific place while performing their service. On the other hand, elemental beings of the four elements are always associated with their home holon.

- The beings of the fifth element appeared during the first phases of the Earth transformation process that was mentioned in Part 1. They can be understood as transformed beings previously belonging to one of the four elements.

- Their task is not to substitute for the beings of the classical four elements in their service, but to work on transforming the space and time dimension in accordance with ongoing Earth changes and human transformation.

- In contrast to the classical environmental beings who tend to be introverted (focused on their specific task in nature), the beings of the fifth element are extroverted. They seek communication with human beings and are ready to collaborate with us.

- They reflect the new facet of Earth consciousness that has become sensitive to the tragedy of human beings caught in our rationalistic world creation. Therefore the "new" elemental beings are capable of approaching the physical level of reality very closely and of reflecting the true nature of human beings. They tend to remind us of who we really are.

- The basic frequency of this new generation of elemental beings can be associated with the qualities of love and curiosity.

Example 1
Studying the different roles of the new generation of elemental beings, I observed a being that presented itself as an "information carrier of the Earth consciousness." The new generation can be distinguished from the classical one through a special kind of brilliant white light associated with them in different ways.

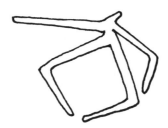

Example 2
This example shows another being of that group, who called itself "communicator." In both cases it is obvious that the spirits are presenting their identity through their form.

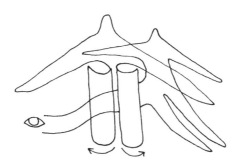

Exercise
Here is an exercise that I propose for perceiving elemental beings
of the new generation. Imagine that the upper part of your body
is composed of two vertical cylinders, and each one moves in its
own direction. They do not touch each other, so there is a very
narrow fissure between them. Imagine standing behind your body,
and glide through the fissure to the front and perceive.

Demons of the over-materialized world

In studying the world of consciousness we cannot avoid meeting its shadow side. The negative effects of human destructive behavior within the beautiful ecosphere of the Earth cannot simply be neglected—especially not within the context of our study of holistic geography. The shadow side of human behavior is leaving obvious traces upon the face of the Earth as ecological damage. There are also wounds within the landscape organism at the etheric level that perhaps cannot be seen. Yet they influence life processes in a disharmonious way. We will give attention to this influence later in the chapter on Earth healing.

There also exists a complex shadow world in relationship to the consciousness levels permeating the landscape. Since the consciousness of the Earth, environmental spirits, and the landscape is of an emotional nature, its distorted aspect can be detected on the so-called astral level. The astral level corresponds to our emotional level, with the understanding that emotions are understood as a specific language of the soul. Emotional reactions are only a reflection of that sacred language—but often an awfully distorted reflection.

The world of elemental beings and nature spirits does not know any distortion. It bathes constantly in the sweet moonlight of Gea, the Earth Soul. Problems appear through interactions with human beings who have lost the sense of their true identity, and through this loss of identify the sense of justice and love toward beings of nature.

Demons of the over-materialized world are children of the distorted relationship of human civilization with the world of Earth consciousness on all levels. They represent alienated consciousness holding up the narrow structure of the materialized world in which we presently live. They are masters of mechanisms that are and that for quite a long time have been moving the materialized world in the direction and process of breaking away from the space of reality, and of becoming pure deadly illusion. Demons of the over-materialized world can appear in different astral forms, such as:

- "emotional rubbish" composed of distorted thought forms and emotional packages, projected mostly unconsciously into the emotional field of a given holon by alienated human beings;

- conscious or unconscious astral projections by people who strive for power and wealth;

- demon-like beings who reflect the human will to govern the world structure independently from the elemental world and independently from the will of the Earth Soul; and

- combinations of emotional and etheric "garments" left behind by people who did not die in a peaceful and harmonious way. Since these "garments" posses a kind of their own intelligence, they can act in a demonic way.

It is important that we do not submit to fear while facing the alienated world of human miscreation. There is a new generation of elemental beings that are capable of transforming and harmonizing different levels of the alienated world in cooperation with people of good will and open hearts. As a result of this transforming activity, which is intensifying, the demonic world which propels the over-materialized reality can be considered a disappearing world. Outwardly it may still look strong and powerful, but seen inwardly it is quickly losing its control over the space of our everyday reality. (Details may be found in the chapter on 9/11/2001 in my book *Turned Upside Down*.)

3.6 Manifested forms of landscape

There are some spiritual teachings that consider material reality as the densest expression of the divine light, representing the lowest level of the evolutionary scale. Just the opposite! From the geomantic point of view, divine light takes part in the process of incarnation. Divine light not only inspires the subtle levels of the cosmos but also permeates its densest level, the material dimension. In this sense life manifested within matter represents the peak of the evolutionary process, perhaps the most holy expression of divinity.

The beauty and strength of the material dimension of reality can become lost under the pressure of mental concepts that tend to separate and break it away from the organism of vital energies and to disconnect it from the inspirations of Gea-consciousness. As a consequence human beings find themselves within an over-materialized world which can properly be considered a world of illusion. To sustain the material world as the most precious expression of light and to avoid ecological and spiritual deterioration, we need to work firmly on reconnecting with the invisible dimensions of reality and the soul powers of Gea.

The holographic language of forms

There are many aspects of the physical landscape that appear important for geomantic exploration. For example, consider the mineral structure of the ground. If the ground of an area is composed mainly of granite layers, the quality of that landscape will be different as compared to an area with chalk underground layers. Chalk is an organic material derived from ancient sea organisms, is feminine in its characteristics, and is capable of supporting life processes in their relationship to the underground. Chalk layers allow water to sink down into the depth of the Earth. Granite works in the opposite direction. Originating from the Earth core, granite is capable of conducting impulses of the Earth Soul to the planet's surface.

Another aspect of the materialized landscape to consider is the shape of its forms. Broad dish-like valleys are feminine in their character. They concentrate powers of life and give opportunity to them to express fully. Mountainous slopes with rocks and precipices are masculine in their quality. Radiating out, they usually represent the Yang aspect of the given landscape.

Yet looking at the shape of physical forms may not be enough. Each form by its own nature is radiating. By the expression "holographic language of forms" we mean that even if landscape forms appear to the outer senses as pure physical forms, they comprise all other dimensions of the multidimensional reality, which tend in one way or another to find their expression through the physical shapes. Often in geomantic work corresponding geographical maps are used to explore the radiation quality of landscape forms that are too large to be explored directly "on the ground."

A third important geomantic aspect of the materialized landscape is its horizon, especially the points of sunrise and sunset. Exact scientific measurements have demonstrated that many sanctuaries of nearly all cultures worldwide are positioned in relationship to the points of sunrise or sunset in combination with specific dates of the year's cycle. The point of sunrise on the horizon may symbolize the relationship between the Earth holon and the next larger holon, the holon of the solar system with other worlds, or with the relationship between Heaven and Earth. The point of sunset can be understood as a point of relationship to the underworld and the world of ancestors. In addition, the shapes of mountains or hills that appear on the horizon can provide indications for the importance or identity of a given place.

SCHRECKHORN PEAK

STOCKHORN LOOKS LIKE A HUGE SPHINX

THE SOFT FORMS OF LÜSEBERG

Example
While positioning lithopuncture pillars (a form of Earth acupuncture) at the place called Ruettihubelbad, Switzerland, I discovered that each of the pillars with carved cosmograms, symbolizing the identity of the place, relates to one of the three dominant mountains on the horizon. Two of them, Schreckhorn and Stockhorn, belong to the main chain of the Alps. Lueseberg is a local hill.

The essence of rivers and lakes

Rivers and lakes represent autonomous geomantic systems in the landscape. Their holon encloses not only the water body of the river or lake, but it also includes a certain part of the surrounding landscape. For example, let's consider the longitudinal body of a river. From the geomantic point of view, the river is running inside a rounded membrane that resembles a tube. The transparent tube of the river helps to concentrate the river's life powers. Let's say that the tube of the river undulates through a valley. River valleys (landscapes) show a specific geomantic system composed of Yin and Yang power centers positioned in a rhythmical succession along the body of the river. Through their interaction the energy field of the river's holon is held upright. It is this energy field that enables the feminine qualities of a given river to resonate in the environment of the surrounding landscape through which its course is winding.

It is a bit different with lakes. Their health and vital power is balanced and sustained through a system of Yang centers positioned in the surrounding landscape environment of the lake. They have been purposely created by the Earth Soul to counterbalance the considerable Yin power of water accumulated in a lake. This is where problems with artificial lakes originate—since they were created in locations that do not have a geomantic balancing system in place, they exist within the given landscape as a foreign body.

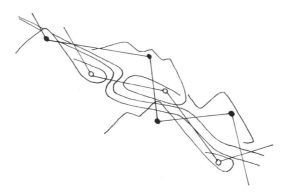

Example 1
This example shows the Yin-Yang structure along the river Sava in Slovenia. The Yin points (white dots) and Yang centers (black dots) rhythmically supplement each other.

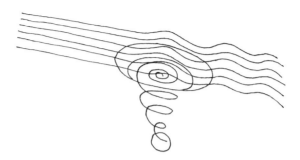

Example 2
Rivers have also their own chakra system. The drawing shows a large chakra of the river Danube that I observed at Vukovar, Croatia. It looks like a hole in the river bed bottom. A spiral of regeneration pulsates within the hole, connected to a vital-energy center below. The water ether of the flowing river sinks into the hole for regeneration.

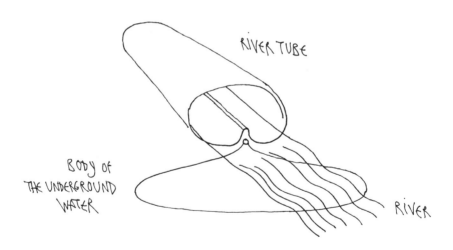

Example 3
This example shows the river tube of the Rhine observed while crossing the river by boat in Basel, Switzerland. At its center in the middle of the river the tube shows an elevation, like a core stripe. It represents the river's connection to the body of the underground water as a basin of the water's archetypal forces.

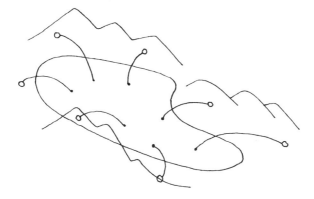

Example 4
This example shows how the wisdom of nature is working to balance the accumulated Yin of a lake with a system of Yang centers positioned in its environment.

Trees, rocks, and caves

Not just grand features like mountains, valleys, rivers, and lakes play important roles at the material level of the landscape. What about sacred trees and rocks?

By growing a knot (knurl) on its trunk, a tree shows where radiation emanating from the ground is of a negative nature, which means that it hinders growth. Developing a protective sphere on the corresponding place, the tree spirit makes an effort to reflect that radiation away from its aura. Or by growing a far-reaching branch that does not fit aesthetically into the crown of a tree, the tree spirit might be showing a source of beneficial radiation, perhaps a vital-energy center positioned next to the tree. Trees growing on sacred spots are capable of developing exquisite forms through which the special quality of the place can find expression.

Holy rocks and caves also reflect characteristics of the landscape. Rocks may appear to be scattered randomly in a landscape, but they may be perceived as having been positioned there through the will of the Earth Soul or through the rituals of humans. They serve not only as markers of sacred places or vital-energy centers. Their position also usually serves to amplify their radiation or presence within a given landscape.

Caves represent a negative counterpart of rocks, the absence of rock structure. As rocks stand for the vital powers of landscape, caves represent the powers of death, transformation and regeneration, or the powers of the other world. They serve as places of communication with the worlds of soul, be it the soul of the Earth, group souls of animals, or the souls of deceased human beings.

Example 1
Above shows a pine tree in an ancient sacred field at Uggarde Rojr, Gothland, Sweden. The place is marked with several ceremonial mounds dedicated to the communication between Heaven and Earth. The lower part of its crown touches the Earth, while the upper part reaches toward the sky. In this way the tree becomes a cosmogram of the place.

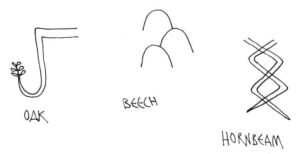

Example 2
At a place of an Interdimensional Portal leading toward the inner dimensions of the Earth, close to Wassmuthhausen, Germany, three different kinds of trees show the symbols of a portal. An oak is growing one of its branches vertically down toward the ground, a beech shows in the bark of its trunk forms of portals, and a hornbeam shows in its branches the ancient symbol of entering other dimensions called "Jacob's ladder."

Example 3
The Geneva cathedral is positioned above an important heart center which has difficulties expressing its exquisite quality. To indicate this quality a rock built outside into the base wall of the cathedral shows an image of the wound called "stigmata" that Christ had at the side of his chest. The image came into being because the rock has iron ore within. Rainwater washed out the iron ore to make the image. Remember that iron plays an important role in the substance of blood.

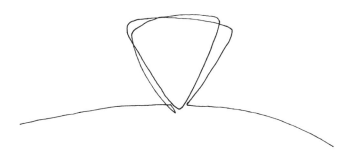

Example 4
Along the southern part of Central Park, New York, there are granite rocks scattered about that were deposited by the Wisconsin glacier. Some of them have apparently been positioned by some ancient culture as sacred rocks. The rocks have been positioned above the granite bedrock in such a way that they hold open a portal leading into the inner worlds of the Earth.

Animal track lines and aquastats

Animals are a living phenomena within a landscape holon. But there also are geomantic phenomena related to animals. These are fine energy lines following paths along which animals move frequently. When an animal or human body with its energy systems moves through the energy fields of the surrounding landscape, a kind of rubbing occurs between two different energy systems. If this "rubbing" is repeated again and again as animals use the same path, an etheric line will be formed as a result, a so-called "track line." The track line remains long after animals may have ceased moving along this same path. The line has become part of the geomantic organism of the landscape. The lines are located about 80 cm above the ground.

One can also find similar track lines along the paths traversed by people over centuries. Human track lines have a special quality if they follow an ancient pilgrimage path. Prayers, together with the spiritual intent of pilgrims, transform a simple line into a ceremonial track line. However, track lines do not occur along motorways or other roads with motorized traffic. The mechanistic way of moving through a landscape does not allow human energy fields to come in contact with the aura of the surrounding environment. Thus the creative "rubbing" does not occur. Rather, motorways are rather empty holes piercing through the etheric organism of places and landscapes.

There are other natural phenomena moving through the landscape accompanied by other kinds of etheric lines, called "aquastats." A stream, for example, does not have as intricate an accompanying energy system as a river. Instead, an aquastat may jump around the stream, preparing the proper atmosphere to enfold the qualities of that stream. Aquastats and track lines love to spiral; they are playful phenomena. Quite often they will form side spirals or dance for a while around a stone.

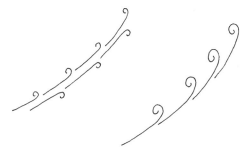

Example 1
This example shows a typical track line along a path where deer move frequently on the left side and where there is a track line established by humans on the right side.

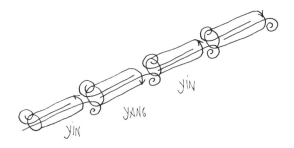

Example 2
A ceremonial path can be recognized by the rhythmical sequences of Yin-Yang polarized units.

Example 3
This example shows an aquastat dancing along a stream as it winds through a forest.

3.7 Gea — soul of the planetary creation

The omnipresence of water

It is almost nonsense to write and read about the soul level in the context of manifested phenomena. The soul of the planetary creation, including its children, the more or less individualized particles of the Earth Soul, cannot appear as phenomena. The soul cannot be touched and perceived, not even at invisible levels.

Yet what can be experienced is a bit more than pure presence. As subtle as breath, the soul presence can be felt. And what can be felt somehow does exist in a manifested way. We find that the omnipresence of water within the disk-like membrane of the Earth surface (or within the animal and human body) can make the soul presence perceptible to our subtle senses—and sometimes it can even become perceptible to the physical eyes.

This means that water—as an ocean of ground water, as a shimmering of rivers, lakes, and oceans, as drops of humidity distributed throughout the atmosphere—serves at the physical level as an organ of transmission for Gea, the Earth Soul, revealing its presence. The ancient symbol of the Earth Soul presence within the fluid organism of water is the archetypal fish. The ever-silent fish within the vastness of the ocean depths is an apt symbol for the way in which Gea is present; for how the Earth Soul in all its incarnation forms can be perceived, all the while as we inhabit the landscapes of the Blue Planet.

Exercise
To experience the soul power of water begin by standing in front of a stream, river, or a lake and imagine turning its water body upside down. For example, a lake will appear before you as a mountain of water. In the moment that the water mass, always hidden beneath the surface, appears revealed, open yourself to feel its presence.

Anima loci — the soul of a place

In exploring a certain landscape or city the omnipresence of the Earth Soul can be identified practically as the soul of the given place. Some languages refer to the angel of a place, but (in a geomantic sense) an angelic presence is something different. Others call this soul presence the "Spirit of the place," following the ancient Roman belief concerning the spiritual guardians of places and homes, called "genius loci" in Latin. According to my experience, the spirits of a place are elemental beings (environmental spirits) that take responsibility for the etheric dimensions of that place. I use a name complementary to the Latin term that emphasizes the feminine (watery, all-embracing, mother-like) quality of the Earth Soul, individualizing as the soul fractal of a specific place or landscape—"Anima loci": the soul of a place.

There also are some alternative terms to consider. I sometimes experience the soul of a place as the "Goddess of the place." This is an expression that underlines the sacred dimension of the soul of the landscape and nature. This phrase also clearly reminds us that in contacting the soul of a place we are not dealing with a separate soul essence, but with a holographic particle of the all-Earth Soul, Gea, the Goddess.

The presence of anima loci can be detected and experienced in different ways:

- The soul of the given place can reveal itself through a dream, or perhaps through an unusual chain of events that we experience while visiting the place.

- Anima loci, the soul of a place, can use the body of someone exploring a place to "enter it" through the means of resonance, and to demonstrate correspondences with the landscape that is being explored.

- There usually exists within the etheric structure of a place several locations or points through which the anima loci tends to spread its influence upon the place's evolution. Those points have some special meaning for that place. They can represent key symbols of the place. They can act as a general acupuncture point from which all extensions and dimensions of the place can be reached.

Example 1
The soul of a place called Regensburg, Germany, appears upon the medieval portal of the city as a carving representing a horned Goddess. Above it stands Saint Ulricus, securing the Christian context of the presentation.

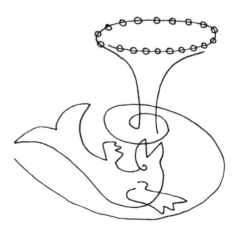

Example 2
While leading a workshop on the soul level of Vienna, Austria, in the lower Belvedere Park I came across a fountain with the archetypal fish represented at the top. It turned out that the spot leads to the place of the soul, if one dives down into the fountain and passes through a narrow funnel rimmed with light balls.

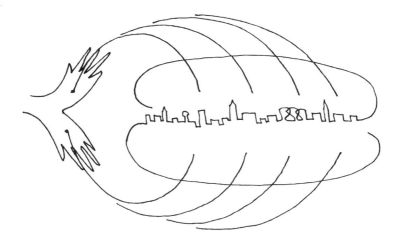

Example 3
While leading the same workshop, the anima loci of Vienna showed me how it tries to reach its city from two levels at once: one from the underground up, and one from the high atmosphere down.

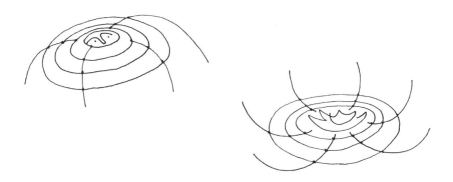

Example 4
This example shows two complementary focuses of the soul of Buenos Aires, Argentina, both found in the Botanical Gardens. The left one shows the anima loci reaching down toward the city, the right one works through the underground level.

Places and paths of ancestors

To understand the relationship of the individual human souls to the landscape holon, it is of central importance to consider the contacts between the two halves of human evolution that we described in Part 2. The world of the soul, usually called the world of ancestors and descendants, represents the invisible part of humanity. Incarnated human beings on the physical Earth embody its counterpart, the visible part of the human family. Both parts are in the process of constant exchange. Both parts are seeking, consciously or unconsciously, to communicate with each other and to find possibilities for mutual exchange.

Places to contact ancestors
Archaeological findings reveal that even the oldest cultures knew places and methods to contact the invisible world of ancestors. What could our modern approach be like? There are funerary places dedicated to the deceased everywhere. Beyond their symbolic meaning they can serve as places to contact the world of ancestors, if purified of inappropriate thought forms and emotions concerning the nature of death. Much more important are places in nature and in cities that are used by the world of ancestors and descendants to spread its benevolent influence upon incarnated life. These locations have a specific geomantic system, similar to Interdimensional Portals, enabling communication between the two worlds.

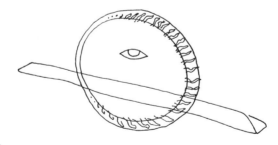

Example 1
A long narrow natural mound called "Rebro" outside Bled, Slovenia, is an ancient place for contacting ancestors. It is permeated by an invisible vertical wheel that is aligned to the mound and turns around the Eye of God. Contacts are being made as ancestor souls move along the wheel and as people walk ceremoniously along the mound.

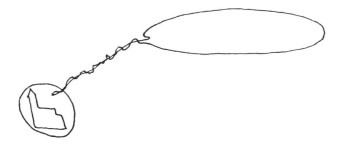

Example 2
The Church of San Sebastiano, decorated with paintings by Paolo Vero-
nese, stands for communication with the ancestors of Venice, of which
master Paolo himself is a most precious one. The church energy field
is connected to the sphere of spiritual beings vibrating above the city
through a kind of umbilical cord.

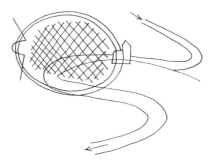

Example 3
Pusti Gradec, Slovenia, around which the river Lahinja winds, is an
ancient sacred place for contacting ancestors. The pilgrimage Church of
All Saints now stands at the center of the half-island. It is connected to
a cave on the other side of the river through an invisible golden ring. A
membrane extends within the ring, serving as a communication device.

Descendants contacting the Earth
Another type of place dedicated to the soul world is concerned with the
process of incarnation. Future generations preparing for birth into the
material world must approach the physical dimension slowly in order
to become accustomed to its dense kind of vibrations. These souls
need places energetically close to the material landscape to accomplish

their preparations. Places permeated with the vibration of the incoming souls were considered sacred by ancient cultures, and were often venerated as places of pilgrimage.

Something similar can be said of places of departure. Human souls, leaving the physical body behind, need places close to the material dimension of landscape to dwell for a while, with the purpose of purifying their etheric and emotional "garments" before they can be recycled by the beings of the fire element. Spaces of this kind are usually located underground (which later gave rise to the partially accurate idea of a purgatory). Such places are not appropriate for contacting ancestors, since the souls there are involved in after-death processes. Ancient cultures sometimes used these locations as places of initiation to provide people with the knowledge of death and reincarnation.

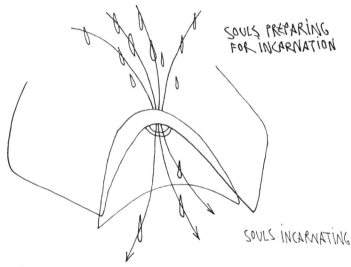

Example
The plateau of Holy Hemma in Carinthia, Austria, has been a place of pilgrimage since antiquity. Located at its side is Rosalia Cave, with an opening at its top that looks like a fontanel, the opening that infants have at the top of their skull. This cave opening is a threshold through which souls must pass to incarnate within the corresponding landscape holon. In my vision I saw a tree above the opening where souls, like drops upon the tree of life, wait for the proper moment to drop down through the cave opening and proceed toward the mother's womb.

Paths of the soul

Souls who are not presently incarnated are leading a life in the other world. Even if they are without form, they still have their path to learn and to evolve. One of the methods for non-incarnated souls to grow spiritually is to visit sacred places of the Earth at their etheric level and to study knowledge regarding the secrets of life stored there.

To approach such sacred places these souls move along spirit paths called "paths of the soul." Often spirit paths intersect with human creations, sometimes for good or for bad. Some change in the configuration of a landscape, perhaps due to some building activity, may disrupt a path of the soul. This change results in a kind of chaos in that place, with souls drifting around and searching for the lost path. Without the clear direction provided by the etheric path it is hard for the subtle soul to find the needed orientation, since it is close to the disrupted material dimension of reality.

On the other hand, soul paths provide an opportunity for souls separated from each other by the veil of the material world to meet, at least in spirit, and to come close and feel the presence of each other. Places where material and soul paths come close are eagerly, but mostly unconsciously, visited by incarnated pilgrims and tourists with the silent hope of touching one of the beloved souls from the other world.

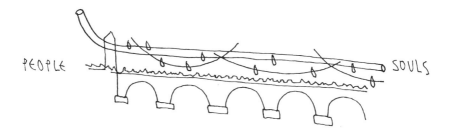

Example 1

The famous medieval Charles Bridge in Prague is a place where a soul path leads parallel to the bridge, about 5 meters above the pavement. The path leads toward the Virgin Mary Loreto sanctuary close to the Prague castle. I observed moments when the soul path was lowered down to respond to the intention for a close encounter. The bridge is one of the most frequented places in Europe.

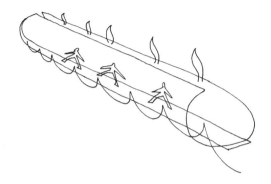

Example 2
This example shows the pilgrimage path toward Santiago de Compostela in northern Spain that I walked in 2004. Seen with the inner eye, the path shows two stories. The lower path stands under the influence of the Earth Soul powers from below, and is walked by embodied pilgrims. The upper path is "walked" by souls and is rich with cosmic radiation.

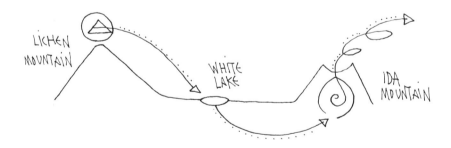

Example 3
The Sushwap region west of Vancouver, Canada, is centered around Ida, a holy mountain and former volcano. Souls glide toward Ida along a path that leads from Lichen Mountain down to White Lake through the atmospheric space, and from there on underground. Ida Mountain represents an etheric library of Earth wisdom.

Centers of discharge

The universe is organized in cycles. It is not possible to store energy without discharging it at some point. That which we, who live upon the Earth surface, do not need any more should be released through the Earth membrane to nourish other worlds that are beyond ours. Within the context of the worlds of the soul and within the framework of the present chapter, we do not mean nourishment in the form of matter or energy. We mean nourishment in the form of soul information.

Water is known as the best carrier of information. Where the soul level is concerned, the body liquids are those carriers. Practically this applies to blood and urine. The blood of sacrificed soldiers changes a landscape for good and for bad. Urine also carries soul information down through the Earth membrane. A cycle is put into motion with the release of these liquids into the Earth, a cycle whose arc eventually returns to the Earth surface, and which blesses our incarnated life.

Analogous to the human discharge system, the landscape also has centers of discharge. Upon observing their forms, one is challenged to discuss them in the chapter on vital-energy centers. But their relationship to the underground soul life is too obvious.

Centers of discharge look like etheric vortexes sucking in depleted energies from the surface of the Earth. They can be considered as the "urine" of a given landscape. Moving downward through the vortex structure of the Earth, the "urine" of the landscape undergoes a distillation process so that pure soul information arrives into the underworld. It is the soul information of living beings breathing, communicating, and loving each other at the surface membrane of the Earth. The drops of distilled information are gathered by etheric rivers that flow underground, nourishing its soul life with the soul information distilled from the "upper" life sphere.

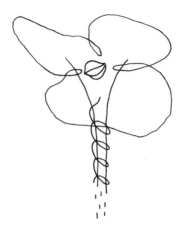

Example 1
This example shows a discharge center with a kind of sucking mouth at its center. It "sucks in" depleted energies ready for discharge.

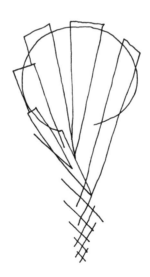

Example 2
This kind of discharge center pulls depleted energies into a distillation process.

3.8 Phenomena of the changing Earth

With this new chapter the course of our narration makes an important shift. Previously our attention was directed toward geomantic phenomena that enable the landscape and its beings to breathe and to evolve according to their blueprint, according to their flow of life. Now we are going to consider phenomena which are primarily aimed at bringing about changes, or enabling the Earth Cosmos to change. As explained in the first part of the book, the Earth is already taking part in the process of global change. The effects are widely known, with the worldwide media reporting on such news as climate change, global warming, unprecedented storms and fluctuations in the seasons.

From geomantic point of view, Earth changes are a consequence of a much more profound transmutation process that may lead toward a "new Heaven and a new Earth," as expressed in the words of the Revelation of Saint John, an ancient book widely known as the Book of the Apocalypse. The prophecy of the Apocalypse, translated into current terminology, means that a new Earth Cosmos is about to emerge through processes underlying current Earth changes. This Earth transformation process leads to a new constitution of the space of reality, where the earthly (material) and cosmic (spiritual) aspects of reality are not separated from each other but united through a synthesis.

Geomantic phenomena of the changing Earth represent tools that Gea, the Earth Soul, is using to bring about desired changes at the surface of the Earth. It is important to note that we can use complementary approaches and methods to help human beings change and attune to the current Earth changing process. They are not the subject of the present book, but detailed information can be found in two other books I have written, *Turned Upside Down* and *Touching the Breath of Gaia*.

Interdimensional Portals

The most challenging aspect of the Earth Change process underway is that of opening the narrow space of reality that is presently limiting the free interplay between different dimensions of space and time. A conscious wall of energy is being maintained between the so-called visible and invisible dimensions of reality. Regardless of which side of the wall one exists on, there does not appear to be much opportunity to confer or cooperate with the other side.

Interdimensional Portals are geomantic organs that make exchange between different dimensions of reality possible. Before the Earth changes came into motion this geomantic system of Interdimensional Portals was asleep. The reappearance of Interdimensional Portals means that the unprecedented transformation of the rationally structured space-time dimension into an open multidimensional reality is at hand.

Interdimensional Portals can be considered to be translators of space and time into other dimensions. They can appear as small "pocket" devices serving as translators for micro-ambiences, or gigantic chakras ready to work as translators on the planetary scale.

Within the framework of the multidimensional world, linear time must be translated into another dimension of time. Linear time that functions exclusively within the material dimension needs to be translated into the language of "creative time," a time structure that is a by-product of any creative process. The hallmark of this new "creative time" is that there is as much time available as needed for a specific creative act.

In regards to translating space into other dimensions, the orthogonal space structure used in our culture is adapted for use within the material dimension. The task of Interdimensional Portals is to facilitate the translation of this structure into other dimensions that have equal status within the framework of pluridimensional space.

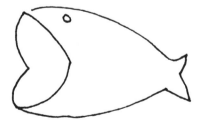

Example 1
While exploring an Interdimensional Portal in the valley of the River Kolpa, Slovenia, the archetypal fish, representing the Earth Soul, appeared to me embodying the function of the Portal.

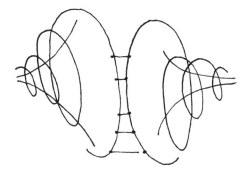

Example 2
The Prague Interdimensional Portal is composed of two discs with spirals leading into other dimensions. The edges of the disc with the dots refer to different aspects of the manifested world that can be objects of translation. The portal is located at the River Vltava, close to the Charles Bridge.

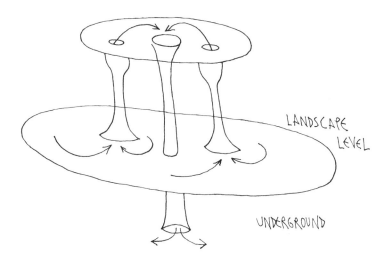

Example 3
A planetary Interdimensional Portal is located in Turkey, in the area between the ancient cities of Laodicea and Ephesos, two of the seven cities quoted at the beginning of the Revelation of Saint John. It is composed of an etheric plateau lifted high above the landscape and three funnels serving as translators.

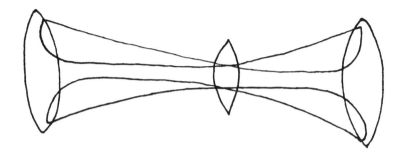

Example 4
This example shows the acceleration channel connecting the front and the back chakra of the human heart in its function as an Interdimensional Portal.

Islands of Light

Equally interesting is another phenomenon of the changing Earth, Islands of Light, which parallel the function of Interdimensional Portals. Islands of Light appear on places that are pure and peaceful, mostly in natural environments, but sometimes also in cities. Islands of Light represent seeds of the new Earth and cosmos, the seeds of the new pluridimensional space that I call the Earth Cosmos.

Islands of Light can be compared with an embryo within the mother's womb. The mother can be identified as Gea, the Earth Soul, and her womb considered identical to our current space of reality. Therefore as ugly and unfriendly as our present reality may appear, it should be considered as a blessed space capable of bringing the seeds of future Earth Cosmos to fruition.

A seed carries inside its microcosmos the whole wealth of the future tree. An Island of Light holds inside its sphere all the qualities of the future Earth Cosmos, even if they are not yet manifested in any way. These qualities exist as intuitions of the character of the yet unborn new reality. Islands of Light appear as extremely subtle light spheres enclosed within their own holon. They appear, disappear, and manifest in other places. They may be small or large. Yet even if they are small, at the same time they comprise the grand whole of the future Earth Cosmos.

Islands of Light can be distinguished from similar geomantic phenomena by these characteristics:

- Their nature is crystalline and not emotional, even if they do provoke strong emotions, like the feeling of having arrived home.

- All Islands of Light are one. At the same time everything belonging to the new Earth Cosmos is present within each one of them.

- The light of which Islands of Light are composed is brilliant, even if it is vibrating peacefully.

Loosening balls

Small "loosening balls" are similar to yet different from Islands of Light. They occur randomly as phenomena of the changing Earth. They look like soap bubbles that have levitated through the Earth membrane to appear at its surface, usually in groups. My sense is that they function as loosening devices, to soften the dense material crust of places and ambiences. In this way they support the transmuting processes of the manifested world.

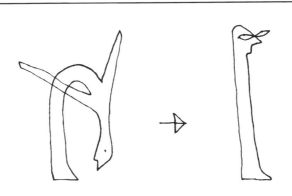

Exercise
To be able to perceive Islands of Light and other phenomena of the changing Earth, I propose the following exercise. In your imagination, bow down to touch the ground with your forehead. Then imagine lifting yourself upright, watching or feeling without hesitation.

Earth Stars

Another geomantic phenomena that slept before the current Earth changes began is composed of several centers, each different from another. These phenomena are located within a given holon similar to the way in which stars are located in the night sky to form distinct constellations. The second reason why I call them "Earth Stars" is that they obviously originate in the inner cosmos of the Earth Soul.

As an example from Ljubljana (the capital of my country, Slovenia) shows, an Earth Stars constellation is usually composed of seven (or nine) energy centers clustered in a constellation that extends approximately one mile long across the city structure, or in other cases, throughout the landscape. This example is published in Chapter 39 of my book *Touching the Breath of Gaia*. (At that time I had not yet invent the expression "Earth Stars." I thought that centers of this kind represent a special form of archetypal sources of energy.)

The main characteristics of Earth Stars energy centers is the role that they play in the process of the Earth changes, including the transformation of human civilization. On one hand they can be understood as a self-healing system of the Earth, since they provide "enzymes" that make all kinds of transmutation processes possible. On the other hand the Earth Stars centers reveal themselves as a set of correlation points, referring to different areas of daily life and to different qualities that need transformation to become in tune with the new Earth Cosmos.

To provide information about how Earth Stars constellations can be composed, below is a list of characteristics from the constellation from Ljubljana mentioned above (the first one that I discovered in 2002, and updated in 2007). The constellation includes:

- A center connecting all the holon units of the place to the source of transformation. It looks like a solar disc with its rays touching all units of life and permeating them with the quality of hope.

- A center transmitting information and instruction originating from the so-called Spiritual World, the world of ancestors and descendants. The term "Spiritual World" refers specifically to etheric centers used as creative outposts by souls dedicated to human development and the evolution of the Earth.

- A center related to the sphere of compassion and divine mercy, embracing the life of the Earth within the larger holon of the solar system and the universe.

- A center of unconditional peace, peace that emanates from the heart of divinity, and is universal in its character.

- A center of change capable of transmuting negative mental and emotional patterns. It works on the principle of drawing in destructive patterns, leading them through a transmutation process, and breathing out their positive aspect.

- A center that can be best described as a source of healing powers that are pure as the purest spring water. Another expression that fits is the self-healing powers of the Earth.

- A center of love that is conscious of its source and dedication. It works as an all-connecting power touching all levels of the tree of life. It even loves its own source.

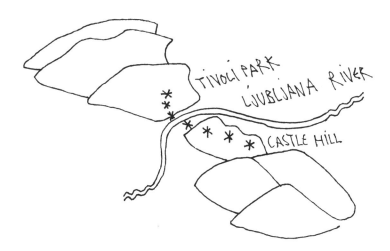

Example 1
This example shows the constellation of seven Earth Stars as it appeared in 2002 in Ljubljana, Slovenia.

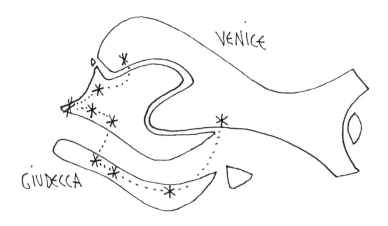

Example 2
This example shows a constellation of nine Earth Stars discovered in 2005 in Venice, Italy.

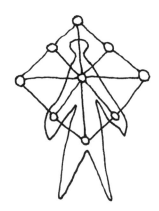

Example 3
This example shows a chakra system composed of nine chakras pulsating at the back of the human body, corresponding to the Earth Stars constellation.

> *Exercise*
> *To experience the quality of an Earth Stars system, imagine a group of brilliant stars behind the back of your head. Then imagine lifting yourself so high from the ground that the stars appear now behind your heart. How does it feel?*

Recycling destructive powers and rigid patterns

The new geomantic systems we have discussed have the task of preparing the etheric body of the Earth for the emerging evolutionary cycle. There is also another "shadow" side of the Earth transformation process, the task of working on transmuting old etheric and emotional patterns of reality that are losing their "raison d'etre." This work of recycling the old one-sided world structure, which has become too narrow to secure a sustainable path of Earth evolution, parallels the need to manifest the foundations of the new Space of Reality.

But to refer to this process as "breaking down the old" would be awfully wrong. There is only one Earth. But energies that are frozen within the structures of the past world are not available for creating the new Space of Reality. Therefore, as powers of the old are recycled (which means returned to their state of perfection), that much more energy can be invested into the new Earth body.

I am aware that this subject is not directly related to the geomantic phenomena discussed in this part of the book, but it still represents a highly important theme that cannot be neglected. The new Earth Cosmos cannot manifest its subtle multidimensional body as long as the old structures are totally occupying the attention of human consciousness and controlling the reality of the Earth surface.

On the physical level the recycling processes appear in the form of natural catastrophes that become unnaturally frequent and severe. Destructive human technologies are contributing to this process. But the physical level represents only the outer shell of a process that is working inwardly to recycle the etheric foundations of the worn-out world. Inwardly the appropriate transmutation process is taking place. The recycling work is related to several levels. They are briefly mentioned below; more material can be found in various chapters of my book *Touching the Breath of Gaia*.

- The transformation of collective mental and emotional patterns that currently are paralyzing the energy fields of humanity and landscapes worldwide. An example of one such pattern is the pattern of aggression that believes struggle between opposing forces is the only way to secure development.

- The detachment from cosmic powers that do not belong to the Earth evolution. The so-called luciferic powers were drawn in by the human will to re-create the world according to egocentric plans. These energies are highly potent and have enabled human beings to build self-centered cultures that are poisoning the life system of the Earth as well as our understanding and actions regarding human gender and the masculine-feminine relationship.

- The spiritual transmutation going on in the realm of genetic codes and the human desire to control the world for its own purposes.

Over recent years the Earth Soul has manifested elaborate geomantic systems to enable a swift process of recycling, complementing human endeavors working in the same direction. Below are some examples.

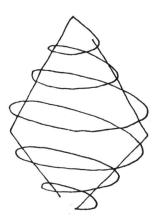

Example 1
This example shows a spinning top-like device of transmutation. It is free to move through a given ambience and to work on the basis of frequency change.

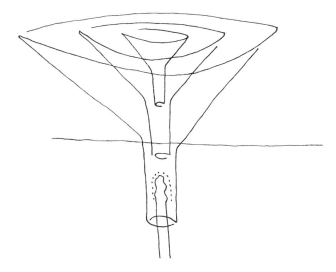

Example 2
This example appears like a series of funnels collecting energies to be recycled and directing them underground toward a potent transformation pillar originating from the Earth core.

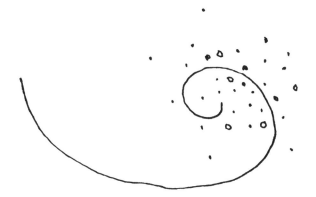

Example 3
This example shows a very strange but effective geomantic recycling system that looks like a bee swarm. It is composed of minute "microbes of transformation" that move around provoking processes of change within the etheric foundations of already transcended reality.

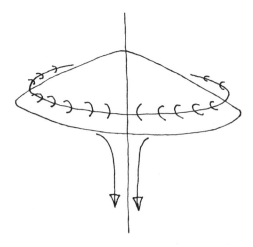

Example 4
This example shows a larger center of transformation. It is built around an axis connecting the dimensions of Heaven and Earth. Its mushroom-like body is sucking in energy units and leading them down into the womb of the Earth to be transformed.

Stimulating units

If we consider the Earth renewal process as all-embracing as described above, the question arises, what happens with "classical" geomantic phenomena, like the heart centers of places and landscapes? Do they stay the same as they have been before, or do they also undergo some basic changes during the current Earth transformation process?

The vital-energy organs of places and landscapes cannot be excluded from the transmuting process of Earth renewal. We already have addressed this question regarding elemental beings, in describing the environmental spirits of the fifth element as the transformed species of elemental beings. Considering the vital-energetic organs like Earth chakras and ley-lines, three venues of change have been observed to date:

- There is a general tendency of vital-energy centers to awaken to their potentials. Many of them were undergoing a slumbering (half asleep) phase during past epochs because our rationally limited, narrow reality did not require much energy to exist. With the fresh breath of change, Earth life-giving systems have begun to awaken and reveal extensions not known before. They are becoming more fully present.

- Vital-energy systems are becoming "more conscious." The difference between a life-giving organ and elemental beings performing their creativity at the given place becomes less, even tending to vanish. Previously the task of life-giving was more energetic; now it is becoming progressively more a function of Gea-consciousness.

- "Stimulating units" should be mentioned. They can be described as secondary centers appearing at the side of some vital-energy centers. Their sole task seems to stimulate the process of awakening an Earth chakra to its full potential. These units appear as a kind of superstructure or additional mini-center within the holon of a vital-energy organ.

Example
This example shows the heart center of Ljubljana, Slovenia. For years local geomantic groups have been working on stimulating the activity of the center. It was recently observed that a "stimulating unit" has manifested there. This stimulating unit is composed of a membrane concentrating the power of the center and a constantly moving and pulsating Energy Star positioned above the center that brings in great dynamics.

The new space organism

It is not yet possible to correctly structure our knowledge about the new Space of Reality because it is still in the process of becoming what it truly is. But it is possible to figure out some laws guiding its way of manifestation. First of all, we are presently taking part in two parallel realities. They are not separated from another, but interconnected. While the old over-materialized world structure is still governing the laws of our daily reality, the new etheric powers and qualities are already replacing its old etheric basis. So we abide within a world that does not seem to have changed at all over the few past years, but in effect it is nearly completely new. Its etheric base has already been renewed.

The manifestation of the new Earth Cosmos will not manifest along the path of linear development. The only way to transform a one-dimensional space and time structure is to become pluridimensional by way of an alchemical transmutation. I refer to the "turned upside down" principle. The universe we see is going to turn inward, to perhaps become a seed for a future evolution, while the universe that we now perceive as an inner world is in the process of turning from the inside outward. This inner world will become our daily reality.

Another metaphor we can use is that of the pole shift. In an earlier chapter we described the correspondence of energy centers to the upper chakras, and provided an example of an energy center capable of serving as a crown chakra, even connected to the base of the spine (as compared to the human chakra system). I also believe that the ice-covered continent of the Antarctic is capable of playing the role that the Arctic is playing now, without the requirement that the Earth turns around physically.

The last chapters dealing with the new etheric organs of the Earth provide information on those tools that the Earth is manifesting now in order to successfully undertake the complicated turn-around process (or quantum leap). One of the purposes of the present book is to give a sense of what a multidimensional Earth Cosmos might look and feel like to help us tune into its essence. Another possibility for experiencing the new space organism may be found in the exercises below.

Exercise 1
Standing upright, imagine having a broad light ring around your waists. Imagine there are many eyes all around upon the ring. Look through all those eyes at once to get a glimpse of the new etheric space around you.

Exercise 2
Imagine that the space around you is round like a sphere, and that half of it is underground. The highest point of the sphere is marked by a point of golden light (solar symbol). The lowest point, the one underground, is marked by a silvery shining point (lunar symbol). Now turn the sphere around, so that the silvery point is at the top and the golden one at the bottom. How does it feel?

Exercise 3
Jump three times as high as you can with both feet at the same time. Then feel around ...

3.9 Cosmic connections of the Earth

Until now our attention has been directed toward all kinds of geomantic phenomena that originate exclusively within the holon of the Earth Cosmos. This time we will open and direct our interest to sources of light and information that pulsate beyond the boundaries of the Earth holon. Our theme concerns the different kinds of relationships that connect the Earth Soul to the wider universe, and the wider universe to the Earth Soul. In other words, we will consider relationships between the inner and the outer universe. Indeed the classical language of geomancy speaks of the relationship between Heaven and Earth.

We can consider different levels while pondering the cosmic relationships of the Earth. First of all we may think of the Sun, the grandmother of our Earth Cosmos. The solar intelligence works from inside the Sun through the means of its gravitational pull to secure the Earth's proper position within the solar system's holon. The Sun also provides the Earth with different types of energy needed, in addition to her own sources, to enable her to develop and sustain life upon her surface membrane.

Another type of relationship between Earth and outer space that we can consider is related to scientific research, which often reveals astonishing results. Astrology can be another possibility for consideration. The subtle interconnections that astrology addresses are relevant to personal and cosmic evolution. Yet these subjects are not exactly our business while studying geomancy. Our interest is focused on phenomena that manifest within the pluridimensional organism of a place or landscape. Let us have a look at some of them!

Angels — holographic units of cosmic consciousness

There is another language that may be used to speak about the consciousness of the universe. Aside from the familiar images of beautiful winged creatures, our traditional language refers to angels as representatives of the divine consciousness. The Greek word "Angeloi" (messengers) introduces angels as "carriers of information"—which brings us close to the modern understanding of angels as holographic units of cosmic consciousness.

The individual appearance of angels as depicted in classical works of art is relative. Consciousness cannot be divided. We describe angels as "holographic units," units of cosmic consciousness. If angelic beings appear as individual units, this is due to a specific task they perform— within one and the same unified consciousness of the universe.

Even as I am attempting rational definitions of the angelic world, we must remind ourselves that our understanding must be complemented with an inner perception of their presence related to the whole of the Earth. Their focuses of consciousness, projected upon different sacred spots within places and landscapes throughout the Earth, are all interconnected. They form a sphere of divine love and wisdom that encompasses the Earth, constantly involved in a vivid dialogue with the core of love and wisdom concentrated within the divine core of the Earth's inner universe.

One of the portals of this constant dialogue includes columns of light that are distributed throughout places and landscapes and that represent focuses of consciousness of landscape angels. The angelic world performs its role within landscapes and cityscapes through the media of such light columns. Landscape angels are responsible for the proper structuring of the spiritual dimension of landscape. Touching the Earth surface and the corresponding landscape at specific spots through their light columns, called "angelic focuses," the landscape angels are directing spiritual energies that form energy axes and focal points of landscape temples and other phenomena constituting the spiritual dimension of the landscape. They are responsible for the invisible sacred geometry permeating the organic forms of the Earth surface. (See the following chapter!)

Example 1
This example shows a system of angelic focuses as a unified organism relating to the Earth core.

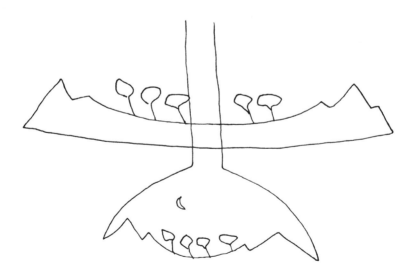

Example 2
The angelic focus of the Mesara plain, Crete/Greece, relates to the stored underground blueprint of its landscape.

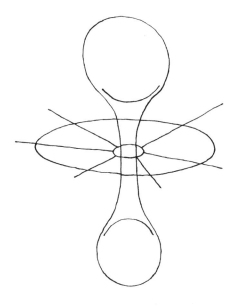

Example 3
This example shows a special angelic focus observed in the Vipava Valley in Slovenia. Above is a center of spiritual guidance, a kind of spiritual monastery, connected to a similar center underground. The connecting light pillar serves as a distributor of information.

Exercise 1
To perceive an angelic presence in the landscape, imagine lifting yourself high into the air. Make a 360-degree turn backward. Remain there, and perceive without a moment of hesitation.

Exercise 2
Next imagine lifting yourself by your feet high up into the air. Hanging in the air with your head downward, open yourself to perception without a moment of hesitation. Ground yourself after both exercises, and give thanks for the experience.

Resonance points of planets and stars

If we are to explore sources of light and information that pulsate beyond the boundaries of the Earth holon, we must consider focuses of planets and stars that often can be detected upon the Earth surface. They have an important role to play in helping the Earth Soul hold its connections to the greater holons of the solar system and galaxy. Using the geocentric world view presented earlier, we can anticipate that there must be a geomantic system that anchors the powers of stars and planets within the landscape membrane. Through their specific radiation they are capable of contributing precious qualities to the geomantic organism of places and landscape. They represent tasty spices mixed into the radiation soup, orchestrated through the geomantic systems of a given landscape.

Resonance points of planets and stars on the Earth are anchoring points where signatures of specific stars and planets vibrate to anchor the resonance bridge leading to the corresponding heavenly bodies. In some cases they appear singularly to enrich a place with a specific radiation. In other cases they appear as "Star Fields," as groups of focuses that together form a complex geomantic organ. Star Fields were often recognized by ancient cultures as sacred places related to their cosmic home or star planets.

Resonance points of planets and stars represent one of the most subtle phenomena to be found upon the Earth surface. Each resonance point is related to an underground vortex that helps to "digest" the incoming information and to translate it into a language spoken by the geomantic systems of the Earth planet. But how is it possible to distinguish which planet is resonating with a specific place? It is possible to recognize them with the help of their signature printed upon the place.

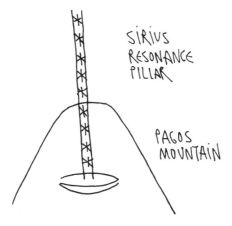

Example 1
The mountain Pagos above the ancient city of Smyrna, Izmir, Turkey, represents a focus of the star Sirius. A vessel-like etheric structure positioned within the mountain acts as the translator to make the Sirius vibrations digestible for the Earth system.

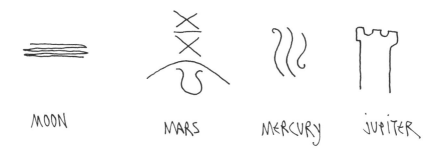

Example 2
This example shows signatures of different planets observed at Cluny Hills, Forres, Scotland. The moon signature resembles rising silvery clouds. The Mars signature relates to the opposition between two contradictory forces. Mercury provides the feeling of being etheric and mobile. Jupiter provokes a feeling of a high and stable tower.

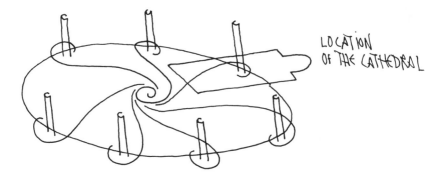

LOCATION
OF THE CATHEDRAL

Example 3
The Star Field in front of the cathedral of Turku, Finland, is composed
of resonance points of the seven classical planets, arranged in a sur-
prisingly geometric way. Since the focuses of planets are interconnected
through ceremonial track lines, one can imagine that the cathedral was
positioned next to a pre-Christian sacred place, where cosmic relation-
ships were experienced in a ritual manner.

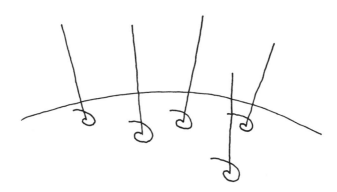

Exercise 4
The resonance pillars of the different planets of a Star Field close to
Eberharting, Bavaria, were probably never used for ritual purposes, so
they show an organic distribution upon a flat hill.

Systems of exchange between Heaven and Earth

Complementary to the Star Fields initiated by sources originating from different stars and planets of the wider universe, the Earth Soul Gea has created her own systems to uphold and to further her relationships with the larger holon units of which the Earth is part. Using a symbolic language, we refer to systems of exchange between Heaven and Earth. But if we wish to be exact, we should name them "systems of exchange between smaller and larger holon units of the wider universe." In other words, the term "Heaven" can represent either the holon of the solar system or the holon of our galaxy.

The simple geomantic system of exchange between Heaven and Earth can be compared to the landscape's breathing system described in Chapter 3.2. This system is composed of centers that absorb the influx of cosmic powers and centers of outflow that are responsible for giving out Earth information to be absorbed by cosmic energy fields permeating the Earth holon. (In the same way that the Earth is part of larger holons, we also are part of their energy fields.) To clarify the difference between the resonance points of stars and planets, centers of cosmic influx relate to general cosmic energy fields, mainly the ones created by the Sun, and not to specific star or planetary holons.

Larger systems of exchange between Heaven and Earth are composed of two three-sided etheric pyramids positioned one above the other. Their ground planes touch each other at the level of the landscape. The two light pyramids are positioned in relation to each other in such a way that their ground planes form the Star of David. The pyramids possess a common axis that represents the backbone of the exchange between cosmic and earthly powers. The peak of the upper pyramid attracts the powers of the wider universe (cosmic powers) and sends them along the axis underground to the peak of the lower pyramid, while the lower pyramid simultaneously sends Earth Soul impulses upwards to be distributed by the peak of the upper pyramid.

In addition, the cosmic impulses that are transmitted down to the peak of the lower pyramid are being distributed. This distribution takes on the form of a spiral that eventually brings the impulses up to the Earth surface, so that they can permeate the large landscape belt extending around the pyramids with their cosmic influence.

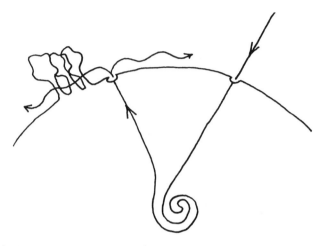

Example 1
This example shows the simple function of systems of exchange between Heaven and Earth.

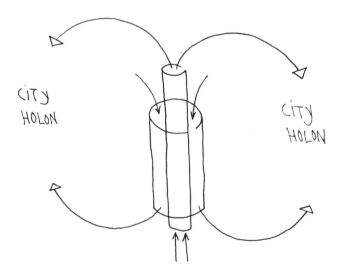

Example 2
Systems of exchange between Earth and Heaven often take on the role of a crown chakra of a landscape. Here is an example from Hanover, Germany. The belfry of the main church of the city is located within a system of exchange that represents the crown chakra for the Hanover cityscape.

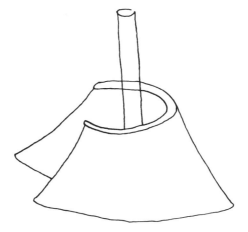

Example 3
The extinct volcano Haleakala, on Maui, Hawaii, represents the crown chakra of the island while acting as a device of exchange between Heaven and Earth. The edge of the crater transmits Earth powers out into the cosmos while the light pillar in the middle directs cosmic forces underground.

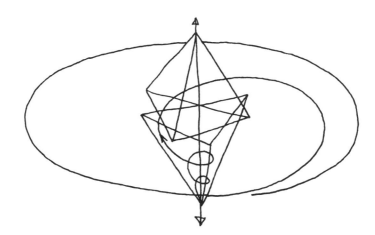

Example 4
This example shows a system I have worked with, composed of a double pyramid located in the landscape of Swiss Seeland between Bern, Biel, and the Jura Mountains. The length of the sides of the pyramid is 15 miles.

3.10 The spiritual dimensions of landscape

After discussing geomantic relationships between the Earth holon and the wider universe in the previous chapter, let's concentrate again on our home holon, the Earth Cosmos. This time we will consider the most subtle phenomena to be found within the organism of a landscape, phenomena related to the divine presence. The Earth Cosmos is centered in its own inner sun, its innermost self, and does not know any other source of divinity but its own divine nature. Divinity is one and cannot be divided among outer and inner dimensions. It always prevails at the center, while simultaneously encompassing the whole.

For too long people have searched for divinity outside of themselves, beyond the clouds, in the vastness of the universe. Our teaching of sacred geography aims at finding the divine presence within everyday reality, within the places where we live—while at the same time each of us aims to relate to our own divine core, as does Gea, the Earth Soul. A new geocentric way of looking upon the Earth holon honors the divine core of the Earth and requires that we find elements of the divine presence in our environment. In referring to the divine presence in the landscape, we speak about the spiritual (sacred) dimension of places and landscapes. There are different ways in which the spiritual dimension can be expressed within our space of reality. We shall examine some of them.

Divine presence knocking at the door

There is no form related to divine presence, not even a fixed pattern of existence. Divinity is free to be and to appear according to its will. The touch of eternity cannot be confined to any form. But certainly there are spatial and temporal strategies through which divinity can best find expression. I find two of them crucially important for the present epoch of change and transmutation.

Orientation turned upside down
Wherever we are, in order not to become lost in chaos and disease, we have to find our orientation. There is a "pole-shift" underway, a change from the heliocentric system of being centered in the Sun to a

geocentric Space of Reality. Speaking in the language of the human body, the root chakra generally takes on the role anticipated by the crown energy center. To say it more exactly, the crown chakra starts to work through the root, and the root chakra performs its task of grounding through the crown chakra.

This means that a new kind of orientation is needed. If the divine presence prevails at the center of the Earth Cosmos, the crown chakra orientates itself downward toward the center of the Earth, to align ourselves to the essence of divinity. If the task of the root center is to anchor ourselves in the space of reality, it must work upward and sideways to ground our personal energy systems. The divine core is downward and the manifested universe is found upwards, where the physical universe is waiting for life to be spread beyond the frontiers of the living Earth.

Exercise
To orientate yourself in the universe, direct a ray of attention from your crown chakra downward toward the Earth core. Vibrantly hold it for a while, while anchored in the Earth core. Then continue grounding yourself. Send a ray of attention from the root chakra upward to the crown, and from there spread a funnel of rays to anchor yourself in the surrounding landscape and in the heavenly arc above.

Divine Couple

In a world where right relationships are broken on all levels, the balanced presence of the feminine and masculine facets of divinity can be understood as an act of healing. In fact, I find focuses of divine parents always appearing in pairs in the present epoch of Earth changes. Depending on the language chosen, one can speak of focuses of Tara and Buddha, divine Yin and Yang, or of Sophia and Christ. These focuses are extremely fine in their etheric composition. Focuses of the Divine Couple may suddenly appear and disappear. Their purpose may differ from place to place, but certainly they serve as a door toward personal communion with the Divine Couple.

To give a sense of how focuses of the Divine Couple work, I wish to describe the Sophia and Christ focuses that appeared to me during the course that I held on the grounds of the Green College in Poultney, Vermont, USA, as part of the Steiner Institute summer courses in 2006. Part of my theme was entitled "Christ Teaching – Yoga for the Twenty-first Century," which turned out to be a good basis for the study group while perceiving and interacting with both focuses of the Divine Couple.

The Sophia focus was perceived as a spiral leading deep down into the inner universe of the Earth. In the opposite direction the impulses of the Divine Mother used the same spiral to reach the Earth surface and to bless the world and every being upon the disc-like membrane of the Earth, with no separation. The Christ focus appeared like a light pillar emerging out of the Earth. From the pillar atoms of divine love and peace were beamed continuously into the environment, and returned for recharging.

Landscape temple of the Goddess

The spiritual dimension can be understood as the presence of eternity within the organism of the multidimensional landscape. Eternity does not need any form to exist. By its pure existence within its space of reality, the Earth was made a paradise. The sacredness of the Earth Cosmos was recognized by human cultures very early in our evolution. These cultures attempted to express and bring into consciousness and visible form this sensed reality, to bring what was unconsciously felt and known into physical reality, recognizing the bounds of the physical dimension all the while honoring the inner, invisible reality of the spiritual dimensions.

Human cultures thus gave form to the spiritual dimension and devised sacred rituals. The most typical means used by cultures worldwide to be in constant touch with the spiritual dimension of landscapes and places included marking sacred places with stone settings and carvings, performing rituals, and walking pilgrimage paths. During that remote time the spiritual dimension was translated step-by-step into the form we now call a "landscape temple."

Landscape temples are invisible spatial compositions pervading places and landscapes. No energy or emotional power is involved. They involve the pure spiritual orchestration of different power centers, focuses of elemental beings, sacred mountains, and so forth, through which a supra-structure is formed, capable of holding eternity present within space and time structures.

Neolithic cultures worldwide are responsible for formulating the sacred dimension of the Earth Cosmos. This achievement was made possible through the ability of those cultures to live for millennia in peace and in communion with nature, the elemental world, and the sphere of spiritual beings that included a line of ancestors and descendants. Under such conditions Neolithic people were guided to recognize the deeper meaning of places and their sacred relationship within their given landscape. They impregnated the Earth surface with landscape temple structures that even today represent the basis of the sacred layout of places and landscapes.

Due to the language used by Neolithic cultures, landscape temple compositions are structured according to the threefold Goddess principle, explained earlier in the second part of this book. Later patriarchal cultures used another language and worked hard to adjust the existing landscape temples to their theologies. These later cultures were not capable of creating new landscape temples because of their limited relationship to the wholeness of the Earth Cosmos. They only could subdue—often forcibly and by using black magic—and transform the traditional landscape temples of the Goddess. This applies to all of the Christian, Buddhist and Islamic cultural periods.

Landscape temple structures have become more and more hidden and alien in relation to their original purpose and layout as a result of all these transformations. But their original imprint within the etheric and emotional fields of places and landscapes has not been completely lost. Landscape temples can still be identified in situ with the help of geomantic knowledge, symbol decoding, and holistic perception. The same language of the Goddess can be used to understand how divine spirit works in a given place or landscape. We should feel free to use the language of the Goddess landscape temple in order to anchor the spiritual dimension within the space of our reality again.

How a Goddess landscape temple is structured
Basic to the landscape temple composition is its axis of breath. We do not mean the kind of etheric breathing systems presented in an earlier chapter (Part 3, Chapter 2). In the case of landscape temples, we will instead speak of the flow of divine breath. At its point of inbreath, a landscape temple breathes in the breath of the cosmic holon, of which the Earth holon is but a part. At the point of outbreath, the collected wisdom of the landscape temple carried by the divine breath is distributed back to the wider universe, the Earth Cosmos included.

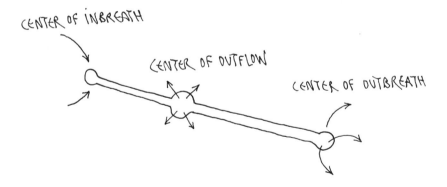

Scheme 1
This drawing shows an axis of divine breath representing the back-bone of a landscape temple. The function of the "center of outflow" is explained below.

The composition of the landscape is made possible because the divine breath does not flow directly from the point of inbreath to the outbreath. During its course through a given landscape, the divine breath branches out according to the threefold principle of the Goddess. It is distributed along three main axes.

- The Axis of Wholeness (axis of the Virgin Goddess, or the White Goddess) supports all aspects of life that are striving toward all-connectedness and universal harmony.

- The Axis of Creation (axis of the Partner Goddess, or Red Goddess) furthers creative processes enfolding within a given place or landscape. Its characteristics is the feminine-masculine (Yin-Yang) interaction.

- The Axis of Transformation (axis of the Transmutation Goddess, or Black Goddess) stands for processes of decay, transformation, and regeneration going on within a given holon.

It is important to note that the axis of divine breath is usually identical with the Axis of Creation. They interact, and the dominant point of their interaction is called the "center of outflow" where the blessing of the landscape temple is shared with all dimensions of a given place or landscape.

The center of outbreath, on the other hand, serves as a place of sharing information about life processes within the holon (through which the divine breath flows) with the wider cosmos.

Another aspect to note is the infinite variability of the basic landscape temple model. Landscape temples of the Goddess can be structured in many ways to adjust to specific geographical configurations, or to respond to special task that the given holon performs within a greater scheme. They can also be created in our present day in a ritual way if the basic intention vibrates in harmony with the divine blueprint of the given holon. The spirit of divine breath is free to respond when the constellation fits.

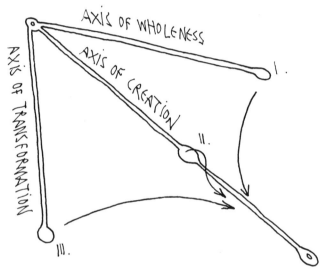

CENTER OF INBREATH

AXIS OF WHOLENESS

AXIS OF TRANSFORMATION

AXIS OF CREATION

I.

II.

III.

CENTER OF OUTBREATH

Scheme 2
This drawing provides a general idea of how a landscape temple is
structured.

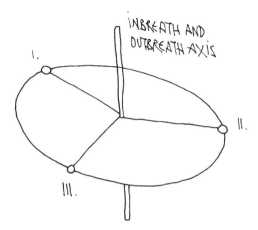

Example 1
Sometimes the axis of inbreath and outbreath is positioned at the center of the holon, with the three Goddess focuses at its edge.

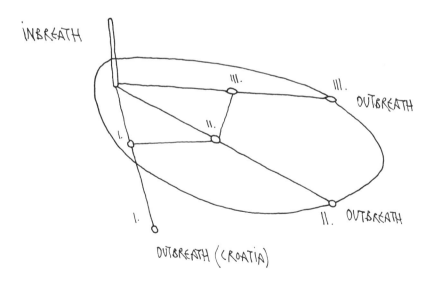

Example 2
Within the landscape temple of Slovenia the highest mountain in the Julian Alps, Triglav, serves as its inbreath center. Each of the three axes of the landscape temple has its own center of outbreath.

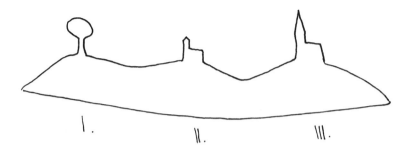

Example 3

This example shows the landscape temple of a former island in the Woerther Lake in Carinthia, with the pilgrimage church Maria Woerth showing traces of an ancient landscape temple articulated in a Christian language. The pilgrimage church stands upon the center of Transformation. Upon the central hill the so-called "Winter Church" represents the center of Creation. A large linden tree stands at the place of Wholeness.

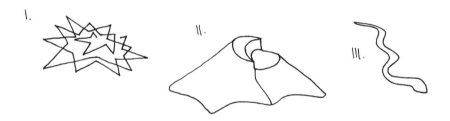

Example 4

This example shows symbols of the Neolithic landscape temple in the area of Gloucester, England. The Gloucester Cathedral stands at the center of Wholeness, marked by an etheric star-like structure encompassing the cathedral. The focus of Creation is centered on the Robin's Wood Hill with a moon-shaped ritual space at its top. Chosen Hill near Tewkesbury stands for Transformation. An earth snake mentioned previously was created here with an acceleration channel at the top.

Infinite tri-partition of the landscape temples

How are landscape temples able to cover places, landscapes, and continents without falling apart into disconnected units? The secret of creating one single whole out of an infinite number of units is: smaller temple structures fit into greater ones following the law of the infinite tri-partition of the Goddess. Any of the three principles always includes all three aspects of which each one knows its own tri-partition, and on infinitely.

Mentally created sacred structures

In addition to the landscape temples of the Goddess created by the Neolithic cultures and their later transformations, there are other sacred structures vibrating throughout landscapes at the spiritual level. They were created by past cultures in accordance with their beliefs and spiritual practices. Partly they exist as imprints into the etheric fabrics of places and landscapes, and partly they are stored within their memory. Alignment axes between sacred sites are an example, which British geomancers call "ley-lines." Also, today, when networks are created and sustained by different groups and individuals, fine threads of spiritual connections are being woven. Usually mentally created sacred structures have more meaning for the cultures that created them than for the multidimensional organism of places and landscapes.

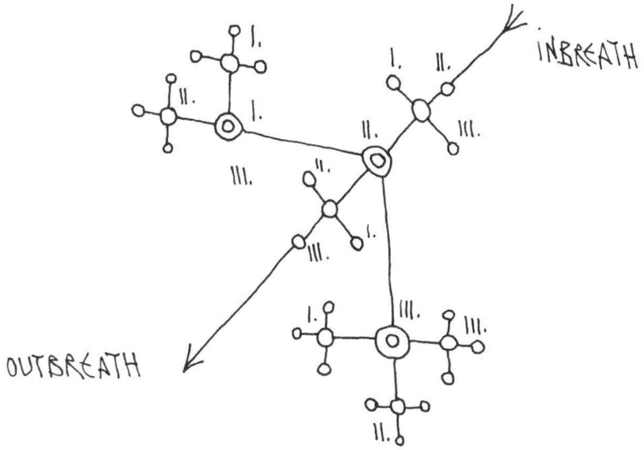

Scheme 3

This drawing shows the principle of the infinite tri-partition of landscape temples. I. stands for the center of Wholeness, II. for the center of Creation, and III. stands for Transformation.

Sacred places reincarnated

Remembering that the course of evolution within the pluridimensional Earth Cosmos is not linear, we may take a step in understanding the development of civilizations upon the Earth. The principle of reincarnation, touched upon in the second part of our journey into the world of sacred geography, also applies to the rhythm of emerging and disappearing civilizations. If we bring to mind again our earlier consideration of the Earth surface as a transparent disc-like membrane, we can imagine civilizations appearing, and then disappearing, upon the Earth's surface.

The Western biblical tradition describes such an epochal change in the story of the Great Flood. A complete civilization disappeared under water, and another one, symbolized by the ark of Noah stranded upon Mount Arrarat, then appeared to populate the whole Earth. The Western occult tradition includes the narrative of two great civilizations that succeeded each other, developed to their maximum level, and then disappeared under the ocean. The civilization of Lemuria is said to have sunk under the surface of Pacific Ocean, and the civilization of Atlantis under the waves of the Atlantic Ocean.

Disappearing under the ocean surface can be understood as a symbol of disappearance from the Earth surface similar to the disappearance of a human being from the manifested world after physical death. But a human being does not disappear in totality. After death the human being manifests its presence within another dimension of reality that we may call the world of soul. In that dimension the being finds conditions needed to continue with its personal evolutionary path.

Following this analogy, civilizations that have disappeared from the Earth surface have not vanished. They are continuing with their further development within the Earth body, or more precisely, within the inner universe of the Earth. But this does not mean that they have lost their interest in following developments upon the Earth surface. They are capable of finding ways to inspire subsequent civilizations. Perhaps more surprisingly, civilizations that long ago disappeared from the Earth surface continue to care for certain carefully chosen sacred places within the materialized landscape. Such places serve as outposts of their parenting activity upon the Earth surface and among successive civilizations.

This explains why some sacred places represent qualities that go beyond those indicated strictly by their geomantic structure. In addition to their own autonomous individuality, they represent a reincarnation of sacred places from "lost" civilizations. They represent a link through which the knowledge and wisdom of the past can be transmitted to the future. Such places and landscapes embody qualities that should not be lost during the calamities that accompany Earth changes in epochs of great transformations.

Often the treasures of reincarnated places remain dormant until their powers are needed in the course of development of the Earth Cosmos. This applies to some major Interdimensional Portals, like the one in Turkey previously mentioned. According to my perceptions it was created during the epoch of Atlantis. Such phenomena are about to awaken now, since they may be needed as devices of transformation during the course of recent Earth changes. In this way the geomantic structures of past civilizations, reincarnated within the organism of certain sacred places, can be understood as another phenomena of the changing Earth.

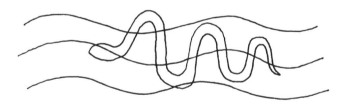

Example 1
My explorations show that at the top of Monte Verita (Mountain of Truth) next to Ascona, Switzerland, an initiation path from the Atlantean epoch has reincarnated. Some of the nine stations on the path were marked at the end of the nineteenth century with carved mythological names. The path has the capacity to initiate people into different dimensions of the Earth Cosmos in relationship to their personal inner universe. A golden snake coiling under water is its symbol. The mountain itself bears the heart center of the surrounding landscape.

Example 2
Jezersko, Slovenia, can be reached through a narrow alpine gorge. At the end of the gorge there was an alpine lake until the fifteenth century, when an earthquake changed the geology of the area. After the lake vanished, three mounds appeared upon the remaining plain that represent focuses of the Lemurian civilization. Their symbol is a bee, which refers to the special Lemurian hierarchical organization and which was adopted by the bees.

Sacred places of nature, animal convention places

Up to this point we have considered the sacred dimensions of landscape in relationship to human culture. Yet there are precious sacred places throughout the world created by nature, which means they are created by elemental beings and nature spirits in cooperation with the worlds of minerals, plants, and animals. So we may speak of "nature sanctuaries" that complement sanctuaries like temples, pyramids, and cathedrals built by human civilizations.

Each place of nature knows it beauty—in this sense the whole Earth is a sanctuary. Yet there are places where a special blend of landscape scenery, coupled with the invisible presence of highly evolved elemental beings, brings forth a feeling of awe in the heart of human beings who visit them. These places have a unique aura smell that allows one to immediately recognize them as a sacred place of nature.

The sacredness of such places does not refer only to their emotional qualities. Usually these places also represent an important center of elemental beings, piloting life processes within a given landscape. Or they are seats of a wide-reaching geomantic organ whose function is sacred to nature. They may also be reincarnations of nature sanctuaries that existed during a forgotten past epoch, where people came together to celebrate the powers of nature or the presence of the Earth Soul.

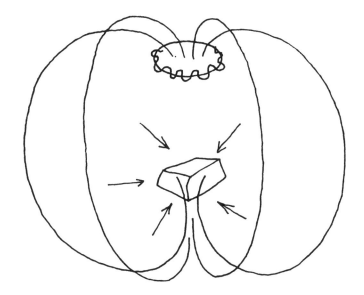

Example 1
During my workshop at Spring Valley College, New York, USA, I visited a large rock in the woods that is sacred to Indian tribes. The rock cooperates with a group of fairies dancing above it. It pulls in the air ether from the environment and sends it down into the depths of the Earth for recharging. At the fringe of the rock's holon the revitalized etheric forces reappear from the underground and are energetically charged by the dance of the fairies. The cycle continues on and on.

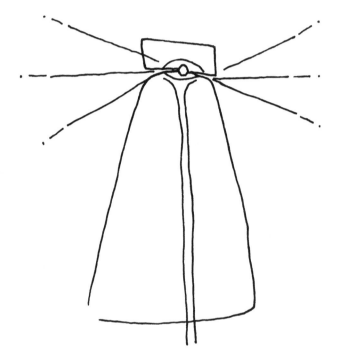

Example 2
One of the famous giant granite rocks within the city-landscape of Rio de Janeiro, Brazil, is called "Pedra da Gavea." It is covered with a horizontal rock layer resembling a human head. During my observation the rock became completely white. Then in the next phase extensive rays began to emanate from the line where the upper layer touches the base rock. There the Eye of the Goddess Gea appeared, signaling that from there she, the Lady of the Earth core, overlooks the surface of her creation.

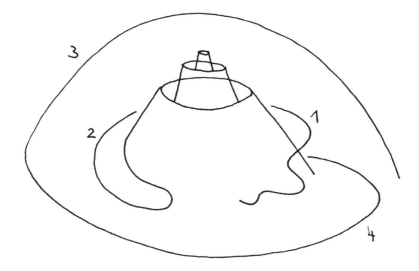

Example 3
During a group perception ritual concerning the sacred table mountain Meissner near Kassel, Germany, the mountain appeared as a majestic ziggurat temple built of gold, embraced by the activity of the four elements(1-water, 2-fire, 3-air, 4-earth).

Animal convention places
Animals represent the dynamic aspect of materialized nature. They move constantly, and not only upon the physical plane of existence. They also know their paths at the soul level. This knowledge leads them to choose places in nature where they meet as family. However, the main reason nature spirits sustain animal convention places is to provide a single animal species (not single animals!) with an opportunity to reinforce their link with the cosmic archetype that they embody.

In this sense animal convention places are related to human sanctuaries which were built for individuals to restore their link with their own divine core. Fairy tales describe sacred places where representatives of all different kinds of animal species meet to talk to each other, as human beings do. To "talk" means that they do not meet in their physical bodies, but through their soul presence. The information that representatives of species are meeting, but not single animals, underlines the fact that animals do not know an individual soul essence, but refer to the group soul of the given species.

Animal convention places can be found at some wood clearings or at places where animals come frequently to drink water. Some of those places are now vibrating within extensive city structures, but they may still be able to function. Not surprisingly, animal sanctuaries can be found at the edge of modern zoos, as if animals are taking care of their imprisoned fellow beings, supporting their strivings to retain their soul link in conditions that threaten their spiritual integrity.

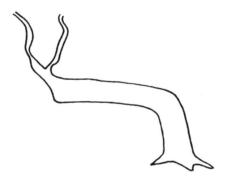

Example
An animal convention place still exists at the outskirts of the city center of Budapest, Hungary, at Toban. One of the oaks in the small park has grown horizontally, creating a figure of a jumping stag. The inn across the road is called, "At the Golden Stag."

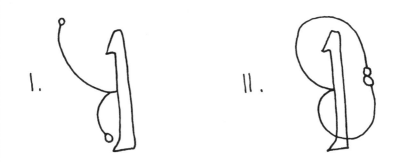

Exercise

Imagine two tail-like ropes emerging out of your navel, with hard ends like animal hooves. Move them in a circle around your body, one upward, the other one downward, so that they meet at your back. Make them produce a strong clap the moment they bang into one another. In that moment, with closed eyes, open your heart for the animal presence, and physically open your hands to receive the animal into your lap. (Prior to the ritual you may ask for a certain animal soul to appear, or you may simply be open to any experience you encounter.) Take your time to experience the animal presence. (You are free to sit down.) To conclude, give thanks, open your hands, and let the animal spirit go.

PART IV

GEOMANTIC PERCEPTION AND EXPLORATION

4.1 Theory of holistic perception

THE FIVE SENSES that we currently use enable us to move perfectly within the structures of linear time and physical space. But if we would like to perceive the multitude of phenomena discussed in the framework described above to the greatest extend possible, our five senses would turn out to be useless. We would simply perceive those phenomena as nonexistent. Fortunately, we do not need to develop additional organs of perception to change this awful situation that blinds us to the larger portions of reality. (It would take millions of years!) Rather, we need to discover a new mode of how to become aware of reality around us.

The tragedy is that present day human beings use the five senses (which were developed in the course of evolution for the exclusive purpose of finding orientation within the material dimension of reality) for entirely different purposes. We often use them as the only compass to find our direction within the organism of life—which in itself is pluridimensional. They are not of much use! Terrified by the possibility of becoming lost in a nonlogical, nonrational, and nonlinear universe, our mind seeks to conceal from us the possibility of combining the rational way of perception with other methods that are no less natural to human consciousness.

Combining our day-to-day materially orientated perception with poetic imagination is one possible way to open our minds. The synergy of combining logically framed perception with the imaginative pull of fantasy can bring about wonderful, unexpected, even perfect results. In this way perceptions can be grounded in a rational framework but also be free to encompass invisible dimensions of reality.

We can also speak of a "gliding mode" of perception. By opening ourselves to diverse levels of information that we can absorb simultaneously, our consciousness is capable of interlacing them into an image of multidimensional reality. Even if we do not see this input or information with our physical eyes, we can obtain an experience of the subtle layers of reality described earlier in our five-dimensional scheme.

While the so-called physical senses are operating at their own level, we have other methods of perception that can function perfectly on other levels of reality. For example, body or sensory reactions can be observed, we can develop the sensitivity of our auras, chakras can be trained to function as organs of perception, and we have the powerful capacities of our intuition to draw upon. But how can we prevent an overwhelming stream of information that could push human beings into madness?

The reliability of multilayer perception depends on several factors:

- First of all, the ethical factor should be considered, as discussed earlier in the first part of the book. The reliability of our perceptions depends on different ethical qualities. How honestly do we wish to meet the real face of the world around us? Are we ready to open our heart and mind to communication in a common sense of togetherness and inclusiveness? How can we expect to perceive the essence of the living world around us if we are not connected to our own true essence? Do we trust?

- Freeing our creative potentials is no less important. Perception can be equated with creation. Prior to the act of perception, a given portion of reality is nothing but a wild assemblage of vibration. The creative capability of the perceiving consciousness gives form to that lot of vibration. If a human being feels obliged to follow only accustomed or culturally prescribed routes, his creative potential will be minimal, as well as his ability to perceive multilayer reality. Perceiving as a creative act can be compared to painting, sculpting, or writing poetry.

- The reliability of multidimensional perception also depends on the quality of interpretation. To understand what we perceive, our mind is challenged to translate images, feelings, and intuitions into logical terms, using the grammar of rational thinking or the language of poetic expression. There are different interpretation methods at our disposal, indeed a whole spectrum ranging from rational explanations to artistic storytelling. Geomancy itself can be understood as a way to interpret the reality and essence of the Earth Cosmos.

- Your heart always knows what is true and what is false. Listen to your inner sense of reality.

Free yourself from mind control

We have often enough stressed the challenge of the dominating mind. Over thousands of years human beings have progressively concentrated upon those tools of perception that operate exclusively in cooperation with the rational mind. As we consequently lost more of our capabilities of extrasensory perception, we became more and more dependent on the mechanisms of our rational mind. This process has resulted in a mind-addicted culture that makes great efforts to globalize this rational view of reality.

To become free human beings once again, and to be capable of enjoying the bliss of the multidimensional paradise around us, we need to find ways to disciple our rational mind to obey the rules of a holistic world view. We have to abolish the dictatorship of mind control—not anywhere else but within ourselves!

The proper role of the rational mind is to help us to master the challenges of the material extension of reality. As human beings we also inherit other aspects of consciousness related to our soul level and the spiritual self that can perform the same service relative to other dimensions of reality. To abolish mind control means to fight like a lion or lioness for the inner freedom to listen to all dimensions of our consciousness, and not only to the rational self. We used to call it "ego," this rationalist self that tends to become the egocentric essence of the modern human being.

There are different strategies we can use to free ourselves from the rule of mind controlling our perceptions:

- Train yourself to perceive the whole reality faster than the mind can set its controlling mechanisms in operation. Be present and perceive instantly. After the act of perception is accomplished, the mind is welcome to offer its interpretations. Persist on a natural course of perception that always gives priority to the whole before any dissection can begin. Train your mind to wait until the right moment for it to offer its capacities—but do not suppress the mind. The rational mind represents (or should represent) a guaranty of our freedom to choose and to change.

- Listen to the child within. Children are allowed to play, imagine, dream, and follow their intimate fantasies. Since we are also soul beings after we incarnate, we never lose our participation in the ocean of infinity. Therefore, we never cease to be little children. To be a child always and forever is one of our basic human rights. Make use of that right and allow yourself to be open to dimensions of reality that your mind may underestimate or dismiss as childish. Be a playful child at the same time that you are a fully responsible adult.

- Renounce esoteric, mystical, or occult kinds of relationships toward the invisible dimensions of life. Be normal as much as possible while dealing with other than normal situations and phenomena. To the extent that you retain common sense while opening to the "crazy world" of the invisible beauty, the rational mind will slow down and stop bothering you.

Some exercises for freeing yourself from mind control may help.

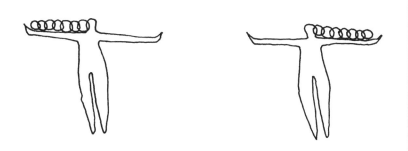

Exercise 1
Imagine your head is a light ball. Stretch your hands out and let the ball roll slowly along one arm. Stop its rolling with your hand, change the direction, and let it roll back to its place. Let the ball roll along the other arm in the same way. Repeat it two or three times. While it is rolling the ball should be touching the arm at all times.

Exercise 2
Imagine that your controlling mind resembles a gray web wrapped around your body. With both hands push the web of mind control aside and immediately perceive the world in front of you.

Exercise 3
Imagine yourself as a little child playing in the garden. Choose a
moment when the child notices you and starts to run toward you.
On the way the child stumbles and falls hard. You go to the child,
lift and press the child to your heart. How does this feel?

Exercise 4
Imagine your inner child standing on your knees. Adjust your view
so that you are looking forward through the child's eyes—simulta-
neously you become the child.

Attunement, grounding, thanksgiving

To summarize our concepts about multilayer perception, we can say
that no additional preceptor apparatus is needed, but simply a new kind
of attitude toward the space of reality. We are accustomed to perceiving life, nature, and landscapes as objects outside of ourselves, assum-
ing the position of a subject that persists in holding on to the famous
subjective-objective distance to the perceived phenomena.

The holistic method of perception takes the opposite path. To become conscious of the whole multidimensional wealth of life, nature, and landscape we need to become one with their organism. Perception, including all different dimensions of reality, must be based upon an intimate experience of the perceived phenomena. Experience means sharing information. In order to receive insights into the world of other beings and realities, we need to offer to them the sweet experience of ourselves and of our own multidimensionality.

Holistic perception is not based upon division but upon oneness. Even prior to the perception process, it is important to cultivate the quality of oneness, the quality of attunement to other worlds and beings, and personal connectedness.

- The perception process begins with an attunement. Like an instrument that needs to be tuned before it can serve the musician, the human being, as a complex organ of perception, also needs to be tuned before the process starts. In this instance, tuning means reconnecting with your own soul essence or spiritual purpose. Make a sweet effort to be who you truly are. Perhaps you may need to ground yourself, to reinforce your connection to the Earth core. You may need to come to an inner peace. It may take only a split second to get in tune, but the results will reflect the importance of being aware of the first step in the holistic perception process.

- Sometimes the first step is sufficient to attune. In other cases, a second preparatory step maybe needed. We may need to ask for the key. Why? Places are coded to protect their identity and their proper place within the given holon. Sometimes the pristine flame of the perceiver's heart is sufficient to open the door of perception. In other occasions, especially if we wish to enter more intimate layers of a place, we need to ask for the key. The key may be given in the form of a specific quality, a vision, an intuition, or in some other way. The image or quality given can be later used during the geomantic exploration of the place.

- The third point involves asking and thanksgiving. Be aware that by allowing us to have a glimpse of their inner worlds, beings of nature, landscapes, or beings of the universe are giving a holographic particle of themselves to the perceiver—and gratitude is the correct response. Asking to be allowed to perceive may open the path for an unexpected perception. Giving thanks is the best way to let the door stay opened for perception to follow later.

Also look among the exercises listed in my book *Touching the Breath of Gaia*.

Exercise 1
To ground yourself, imagine yourself as a tree. From the top of your head, roots grow down into the Earth, and anchor your spirit there. From the soles (souls) of your feet, branches grow upward to touch the heavenly arc and anchor your life energies there.

Exercise 2
To become aware of your integrity, imagine standing within a sphere of light that surrounds your aura. Move your hands around and touch the sphere from inside. Feel free to dance. Through this personal ritual, the sphere that serves you as a coat of protection is strengthened.

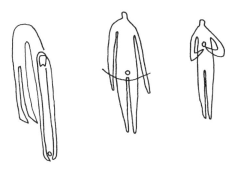

Exercise 3

The purpose of this exercise is to ground yourself in the essence of the Earth within you. Imagine your hands moving deep, deep down to reach the center of the Earth. Take a piece of the essence of the Earth Soul, molding it into a tiny ball. Bring the ball up, and position it at the bottom of your belly. It is a seed that needs time for germination. Be fully present for a moment. Then lift the tiny seed to the level of your heart, open it like a seed opens, and let its qualities spread through your aura field, the environment, and the whole world.

Exercise 4

A simple ritual is needed in asking for the key to a place. Say who you are and the purpose of your exploration. Ask for the key that will help you open the secrets of the place. Open your hands and wait for an inspiration, image, or insight. Give thanks. See how you can use the key during the exploration process.

4.2 Methods of geomantic perception with exercises

Aura sensitivity, body reactions

The magnetic field of our aura is an excellent device of perception. In the same way that our skin has sensors that help us gather information on the body level, our aura field is surrounded by fine membranes that operate not only for protection, but also for perception. Our auras also have sensors that touch on much more subtle levels than our skin does. As we move through our surroundings our aura membranes constantly sense other energy fields, radiation sources, and ambient qualities. Our emotional and vital-energy fields transmit the information gathered to the nervous system of our body.

Our body tends to react to this information with certain kinds of movements and sensations. For example, we bounce on our feet, move our hands to certain rhythms, or feel the concentration of heat at certain regions of the body. We refer to body reactions that help the invisible information gathered by our aura to become visible or conscious. Developing one's own language of body reactions can help bring into consciousness invisible phenomena.

The human skeleton is composed of many joints that are capable of acting as a pendulum. The body can be trained to react to invisible phenomena like a pendulum. Observe the movements of knees, hips, or hands. Counting or tracking the number of characteristic movements may help in this process of developing body awareness. Study the language of your own body. But remember that your body does not move by itself, it is not an automaton. You move within your body. Another way to describe this process is that our imagination is triggered by the sensitivity of our aura and inspires our body to react in a specific way, which in turn enables us to become conscious of the invisible reality around us.

Exercise
Move across a place with your hands in front of your body, touch-ing "the air" in front of you. If you find at a certain point that the quality of the energy field has changed, stop and allow your hands to move or react to that place in their own way.

Chakras for perception

Chakras, the vital-energy centers of our body, perform different functions. They work on vital, emotional, and spiritual levels. Additionally, some of them function as organs of subtle perception. Some of the chakras are equivalent to subtle eyes. Practically, they are capable of gathering infor-mation on different levels so that the perceiver may become conscious of realities that cannot be perceived through our physical eyes.

The heart chakra may be the most important organ of perception—most important because the information gathered is always perme-ated with a precise sense of what is true. Another quality of the heart chakra is that it can help perceive on many different levels. As the seat of our emotions, the solar plexus has a great capacity to perceive the emotional level. Touching a given place with the sensor antennas of the solar plexus may yield the perceiver valuable information. The chakra of the third eye is known for its perceptive capabilities at the soul level, meaning that it is possible to perceive geomantic phenomena as if looking at them from the level of the soul. One of the elemental chakras, the one between the knees, is excellent in perceiving the world of elemental beings.

Exercise 1
Be fully present within your heart for several moments. When you are ready, open your heart to your surroundings and perceive.

Exercise 2
Imagine moving behind your heart. Begin to perceive reality in front of you through the crystal of your heart center.

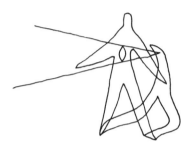

Exercise 3
Imagine that your heart center is a crystal ball with a green point in front and a golden point at the back. Turn the ball around, so that the golden point is now in front and the green one at the back. After the turn has been completed, instantly open yourself to what you perceive. This exercise mobilizes the cosmic aspect of the heart chakra for perception.

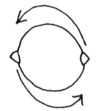

Exercise 4
Imagine that your solar plexus is equipped with very long and fine antennas, like some insects. With these antennas touch the space in front of you and gather information through the emotional level.

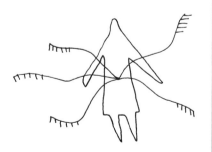

Exercise 5
In order to use the third eye for perception, we need to focus the chakra toward infinity. Once focused in infinity, begin to perceive without losing that contact to infinity.

Exercise 6
To perceive within the world of elemental beings, momentarily focus on the chakra between your knees. Imagine the chakra as a round ball. Then lift the ball into the space of your hips and open it, as a ball composed of two hemispheres would open. Become conscious of your environment in that same moment—begin to perceive!

Turn your back to the place

The front side of our body is well adapted to perceive the material level of reality. In the same way, our back is responsible for perception at invisible levels. The great advantage of our back in perceiving is that it is "dumb" in terms of logical perception. The rational mind has great difficulties in controlling information received by our back. Insights received through the perceptive qualities of the back can be very pristine and inspiring because they are not distorted by mind control. The back can be used as a large screen reflecting the invisible dimension of a given place or ambience.

Located at the back are three pairs of chakras devoted to perceiving invisible reality. The pair at the side of the hips serves to perceive on the vital-energy level. The pair located at the kidneys can be used for perceiving our surroundings at the emotional level. The third pair of the "back's eyes" is positioned on each side of the backbone between the shoulder bladders, and is capable of gathering information at the spiritual level.

Exercise 1
Turn your back to a place and let the place work at your back for a while. Do not judge but observe closely. Be aware of each tiny insight. If a feeling becomes conscious images or words, follow that path of information.

Exercise 2
Imagine slipping behind your back and using the back for looking at the surroundings or environment in front of you.

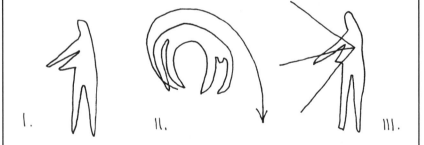

I. II. III.

Exercise 3
Imagine flipping yourself backwards in a full circle. When you are on your feet again, immediately "look" at the ambience in front of you.

SPIRITUAL

EMOTIONAL

VITAL

Exercise 4

This time face the environment that you wish to perceive. Imagine pressing your thumbs on the points that are mentioned above as locations of the "eyes of the back." (You are looking at the place in front of you through the back!) At the moment that you press on the point information will open at the corresponding level.

Intuition, imagination

The imagination coupled with intuition represents the core of holistic perception. Sensory receptors such as auric fields, chakras, back perception, and body movements and reactions provide a large amount of information that our consciousness must instantly address. This wealth of information is of no use if the right-brain consciousness is not capable of sorting and translating it into images that can be decoded by the rational methods of the left-brain consciousness.

Never believe that what you are seeing is identical with what is there "in front of you." Images that may be seen are always the product of a process within our imagination that takes place within the psyche of a person. The reality perceived during geomantic exploration is so complex that it can only be processed through images derived or created by our intuitive consciousness. Typically we refer to inner images, even if all images, even the make-up of our daily reality, are products of an inner process.

Let's clarify further—inner images appear as a response of our consciousness to information received. They may have no value by themselves. They become meaningful in the light of the decoding process. During the decoding process our consciousness, also relying on the feelings beneath the images generated, translates these images into a logical language that can be understood by the rational mind of the perceiver. At this stage geomantic decisions can be made, based upon inner images and feelings. It is this perception process that enables us to determine what kind of phenomena we have perceived. With this process we make our geomantic explorations practical.

Please understand that the level of creative freedom that we provide to our right-brain (intuitive) aspect of consciousness is essential to its ability to form images that are rich enough to catch or perceive the given phenomena in its entirety. Further, the image building process often begins with the appearance of the most subtle emotional qualities. Too often perceivers may underestimate the key importance of these fleeting emotional "winds." If one can be truly open to these qualities, then our consciousness can be provided with information that can be further translated into images. Without this openness, the image-building process may be blocked.

Of course there is another means of perception—multidimensional information that is received from the environment can be translated through intuition directly into visions or images. Both ways are possible, both are valuable. They also can be combined consciously, or, as is usually the case, subconsciously.

I propose some exercises that can enhance our image-building process concerning a specific place.

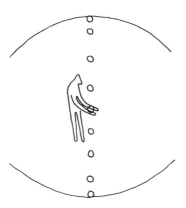

Exercise 1

Choose a point that feels important for the essence of a given place. Stand there and imagine holding a ball of light in your hands. Let the ball fall deep down toward the underground edge of the holon of the place. Once it reaches this membrane, let the ball bounce back upward above your head until it reached the upper edge of the membrane. Let it bounce back and forth a few times, down into the Earth's depth, and back up again. Now catch the ball of light and let it dissolve within your heart space, along with the information gathered. At that moment open to any images and intuitions that appear.

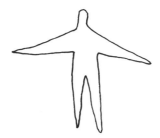 

Exercise 2

Stretch out your hands and arms to embrace (in your imagination) a place, a mountain, a tree, or whatever you wish to explore in its depth. Bring it close to your heart. In the moment that you press the "subject" of your perception to your chest, be open to images and other information that may appear.

Exercise 3
Rest on your knees, keeping your body upright, so that there is pressure on the ground beneath your knees, as if you are applying acupressure to the earth. Look inwardly for feelings and images to appear.

Helpers from beyond

We must also consider the soul aspects of perception. The soul of the perceiver exists at a level beyond the dimensions of vital-energies or the level at which elemental beings can be perceived. The soul level is not involved in perception of such phenomena. Yet another very precious possibility exists. Our consciousness can obtain valuable data from the soul level to help perceive geomantic phenomena at a deeper level. The term we use for cooperation between the soul and consciousness levels is "soul guidance."

By "soul guidance" we mean that the human soul does not have its own eyes to perceive on denser levels, but is capable of guiding our consciousness to perceive with its own perceptive tools in a more complete and satisfactory way. Another even more exquisite possibility exists, the blessing of revelation. There are, of course, different levels of revelation. Its source can be the Earth Soul, the soul of the universe, or perhaps the personal soul. But the principle is always the same. The time and place are right to reveal a secret. The released soul powers are then capable of finding the means to transmit its information directly into the consciousness of a person as a visual or textual message.

In general there are different possible sources of soul guidance. The perceiver can rely on the powers of his or her own soul. The help of ancestor soul beings can bring great results. Special attention can be given to the possibility of elemental and other beings from the soul dimension acting as invisible helpers. In other situations the collaboration of animal souls can be of great value.

Finally, there are fortunate moments when a "perception team" can be called upon. Such teams can be created on a temporary basis or can also have a more permanent character. In these instances different kinds of invisible helpers—many of them mentioned above—follow a person and provide her or his consciousness with insights that repeatedly complement information gathered through the perception routes discussed above. Such teams, consisting of visible and invisible members, can be meaningful and bring reliable results under certain conditions. Namely, no one is "in control"—we all are involved in the life processes of the Earth Cosmos to learn and develop. We respect each other while each retains the freedom of individual autonomy. We help each other because we all share the common wish to serve life and truth.

Exercise 1

This exercise is intended to help perceive the spiritual dimension of a place or landscape. The exercise refers to the "eyes" of one's soul as a manifestation of the triple Goddess. Imagine opening swiftly, one after the other, the Eye of the Virgin, located behind your forehead—the Eye of the Partner Goddess, at the upper edge of the belly region—and the Eye of the Black Goddess, at your back underneath the sacrum (all three face forward). It is possible to perceive only through all three at once. Once the "eyes" are opened, release them from your awareness, and move into the experience.

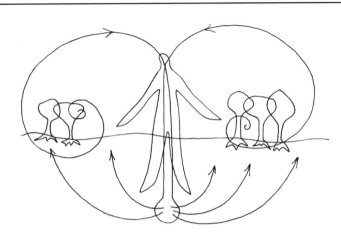

Exercise 2
While standing within the landscape you are exploring, imagine
pulling the features of the landscape around you, one after the
other, through your crown chakra into the vertical channel lead-
ing deep into the soul core of the Earth. Then be still and observe.
The experience of the subtle levels of the landscape will emerge
out of the ground all around you.

Language of symbols, dreams and myths

Up to now we have been considering different methods of perception
that can be labelled "extrasensory," since they do not involve the sensory apparatus used by the rational mind. But equally relevant perceptions for geomantic research can be obtained through logical observation, especially if the observations are combined with an intuitive
capacity that can guide our five physical senses in the right direction.

There is a universal law that we presented earlier as a holographic
principle: what exists at the subtle levels manifests in one way or another
within the material sphere of reality. The problem is that manifestations
of subtle levels that may be perceived on the physical plane are hidden
to our rational consciousness as long as it considers physical reality as
the only real expression of life. Such an illusory view blocks the potential perceptions of the invisible world that otherwise we might perceive
within physical reality.

Miracles can occur once a person allows intuition to play freely with our logically operated senses! Suddenly it is possible to see markers of the invisible dimension within material reality, and to interpret them so that knowledge about the geomantic extensions of a given environment can be detected in abundance. Just look around in wonder and see the paradise manifested within the material reality!

Symbols, dreams and myths may be the most valuable traces of the visible world that can serve as sources of information about the invisible side of reality. They can be seen or read through our "normal" senses. If they are processed through some of the perception methods described above they can serve as invaluable media to perceive the multidimensional reality of places and landscapes.

As in the case of holistic perceptions, symbols, dreams, and myths should to be considered images that need to be decoded and subtly understood within a given context. Yet they have an advantage. In the case of symbols, dreams and myths the image-building process has already been done, either by ancient artists, the dreaming consciousness, or generations of storytellers. The challenge is to catch and understand the key points within a particular symbol, dream, or myth that will help us decode it. Our intuition, coupled with information received from a geomantic perception and exploration of a given place, is critically important. Often decoding a symbol, dream, or myth is equal to creating it anew.

Example
The area of the former Carmini monastery in Venice, Italy, is central to the Venetian Interdimensional Portal. At the wall of the former cloister one can see the carved symbol of two children opening a portal through their hands. The star positioned above reveals its cosmic value.

Negative experiences

It is not possible to deny the fact that we are living in a world that is deeply wounded in many different ways by a civilization that has no regard for the multidimensional nature of reality. As a consequence the actions and emotions of our civilization often damage the invisible world, suppress its geomantic systems, and desecrate its holy places.

If one opens to holistic perception, the environmental scars inflicted on subtle nature cannot be avoided, just the same as with the emotional or physical scars of humans. Yet we should not shrink away or be fearful of this reality. Places and landscapes, or more exactly their guiding intelligent beings, know the ethics of communication. If a person is undertaking a holistic exploration of a place, and if there is a problem that needs to be solved, that place will find ways to communicate. In the instance where more sensitivity or awareness is needed to understand or address the needs of the place, one can always request help and guidance.

The safest approach is to be constantly aware of the quality of one's perceptions. If the quality of perception becomes darkened or blocked, or if one's perceptions encounter a hostile touch, then one needs to adjust the course of exploration and open one's attention to the shadow sides of the given ambience. The information gained can then serve as background for the Earth healing work that needs to be done.

Group perception rituals

There are valuable advantages to working in a group in approaching the complexity of invisible dimensions. A wealth of information can be obtained when two or more people undertake the perception process of a specific place or landscape together. Usually one person alone cannot obtain the quality or accuracy of insights that a group can formulate. The benefit of this approach is not simply to check each other's results. Each person has a different spectrum of perception capabilities. The perception talents of a group of individuals taken as a whole are invariably more diverse and greater than those of a single person, including the opportunity of seeing the same phenomena from different perspectives.

In order for group perception to succeed in geomantic endeavors, the group needs to follow certain rules. To act harmoniously the group needs to perform an attunement at the beginning of the exploration process to request and secure the compatibility of different perceptions. After individual explorations have been concluded, the group conducts a round of sharing in which each participant has the opportunity to present his or her perceptions without the threat or anticipation of judgements from others. After different perceptions have been presented, the group evaluates and explores ways of synthesizing them. In this way some very broad insights can be achieved.

4.3 Exploring a place through the means of geomancy

The act of perceiving a place in its multidimensionality opens up the possibility of gathering holistic knowledge about it. Yet perception does not cover all aspects to be explored. To obtain a more or less complete knowledge of a place or landscape, its exploration should be undertaken on different levels. Below is a series of suggestions about how holistic exploration can be conducted.

Define the holon, or the different holon levels that you are exploring

- Define the boundaries.
- Develop a sense of connection to larger holon units.

Be aware of the natural features within the given holon

- Observe and note characteristic landscape forms (mountains, valleys, rocks, etc.).
- How does water appear in the given environment?
- What relationships are there to the movement of the sun (the location of sunrise and sunset points on the horizon, shadows, etc.)?
- What is the relationship between the Yin and the Yang poles?
- Are there special phenomena observed concerning trees, animals, etc.?

Cultural characteristics of the given place or landscape

- What is the role of architecture (church, castle, city core, etc.)?
- Are there signs of past cultures (excavation places, traditional sacred spots, history)?
- Are there symbols of the place or land (place name, coat of arms, legends)?
- Are there ecological problems (mining, heavy industry, antennas, rubbish dumps)?

Vital functions of the place/landscape

- Breathing (inbreath, outbreath)
- The shape of the energy fields of the four elements
- Positions of vital-energy centers (Earth chakras)
- Channels of vital force (ley-lines, watery [Yin] channels)
- Cosmic relationships
- Places of grounding

Elemental beings and environmental spirits

- Where are their characteristic places?
- Which are their places that have a guiding function relevant for the holon?
- What is their message concerning the place?

Spiritual dimension of the place or landscape

- Find points or places through which the Earth Soul finds expression (Spirit of the place).
- What is the composition of the landscape temple like at different levels?
- Are there angelic focuses?

The health situation

- Does the place feel healthy, complete in its totality?
- Are there energy leaks that can be perceived?
- Are there traumas influencing the emotional quality of the place?

PART V

CREATING THROUGH GEOMANTIC KNOWLEDGE

ADDICTED AS WE are to the material dimension of reality, our civilization is accustomed to operating through a combination of mental concepts and physical labor. Even if mental work is becoming more and more computerized and physical labor industrialized, the dualistic principle remains the same. Mental thoughts, patterns, or plans created within the sphere of our consciousness are projected upon the material world and molded into the desired form. In this way we ignore the continuous universal creative process and the particular role of "our" creation within it.

However, to create within a geomantic framework and knowledge base demands a basic change in our attitude. Why?

- We are dealing with a multidimensional world that possesses its own intelligence. It cannot be manipulated according to our mental concepts and desires. We need to listen to the consciousness concerned and find ways to collaborate.

- We intend to work with subtle energies that cannot be shaped or formed by our hands or even by the most intelligent tools. A new concept of creative work is needed.

- Within the framework of the creative process and geomantic knowledge and practice, it is not possible to remove ourselves from the creative process itself. The creative process always involves interaction, learning, and individual transformation.

Geomantic creativity can be understood as a combination of ritual and practical work. No matter how glorious the results of the working process may appear, if the ritual component is missing, the results are only temporary and more or less unsatisfactory. Within the context of our modern culture rituals are considered to be traditional formalities. They are enacted because of some symbolic meaning attached to them or for the purpose of tourist promotion. Our culture has lost the understanding of the purpose and power of rituals.

This is a tragic and catastrophic loss! Rituals are tools to move energies. Rituals are tools to align personal or cultural creation with the never ending process of cosmic creation. Rituals are tools to make the manifested (materialized) reality real.

Forget about traditional rituals! Each ritual can only be created now, in the present moment, or it is a fake or false ritual. Even if a ritual is repeated a thousand times, each time it is performed the ritual must be created anew. With ritual we create by entering the universal creation process, which does not know past or future. The powers and qualities responsible for the beauty and vitality of our daily life cannot be shaped or materialized by hands or physical labor, or even by the most sophisticated physical or mental tools. Yet it is possible to bring these powers and qualities into our present existence through a perfectly natural way—by performing the corresponding ritual.

We shall refer to "creative rituals"—rituals as tools of creation—to distinguish them from the many different kinds of formal rituals currently performed in our culture. Even if creative rituals are used to perform basic, practical aspects of work, they are necessary if we wish to make dreams a reality. Within the holistic creative process, labor and industry represent the practical embodiment of ritual procedure.

5.1 Tools for geomantic work

Imaginations based on visualization

Recalling the multitude of invisible geomantic phenomena described in Part 3, we ask ourselves, how do we collaborate with their essence for the benefit of life, the planet, and our personal evolution? We know that there are only a few geomantic phenomena that we can approach or engage on the physical level. How do we deal with the other ones? There is a distinct way to move energies and qualities. *Instead of moving them by our hands, one should imagine moving them!* Imagination represents the creative power of the soul, working behind each person's actions and creations. I believe that we could not even move our hands if the driving power of our imagination did not facilitate the movement. To make these kinds of actions happen physically, we first need to create a corresponding imaginative thought or process.

Even when it does not seem possible to move something practically, the imagination is free to act, using visualization as its tool. Some people believe in the power of visualization. But there is nothing to believe. Visualization has no power by itself. Like any tool it does nothing by itself.

However, if the images produced by visualization are driven forward by the soul power of imagination, miracles can happen. Why? Because the power of imagination has its source in the holographic piece of divine creative potential stored within the holon of each human being. It is the power of the divine creative word incarnated within us.

But the results of visualizations, coupled with the power of imagination, can be inadequate if the third element of the creative process is missing—emotional support. Visualization directs the soul power of imagination in the proper direction. Yet its movement through the manifested worlds of multidimensional reality can be accomplished only through the power of emotions. Mental support may be needed, but it does not usually have the driving power that emotions have.

Can you imagine a more powerful tool of creation than love for another being, or love for a special place or landscape? The creative potential of the triangle composed of inner images (visualizations) coupled with the soul power of imagination and underlying emotional energy is immense.

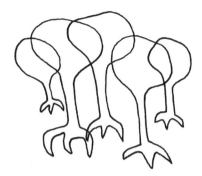

Example 1
While working in Zagreb, the capital of Croatia, we came upon a place that was in turmoil because it had lost its grounding. So I suggested to the group, "let us plant huge trees so that they will take care of grounding the place through their mighty roots." The group then dispersed across the area, each person planting imaginative trees for a period of 10 minutes. The place has subsequently calmed down.

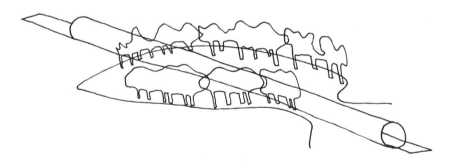

Example 2
Stanley Park is a large nature reserve located at the edge of the city of Vancouver, Canada. To solve traffic problems a motorway was built right through the center of the park. To lessen its disturbing influence upon the energy and integrity of the Stanley Park holon, the working group imagined wrapping the motorway into a light tube. In this way the holon of the park was separated from the motorway route, for which a separate holon was being created through an imaginative process.

Exercise

This exercise is taken from the work with the holon of the European Union (EU) performed with different audiences during a series of ten talks on the EU that I gave while travelling in a circle around central Europe. The symbol of the Union, a circle of 12 golden stars, was taken as the base for this imagination work. The stars represent the individual member states. However, the connecting power linking the member states of the Union to one another seemed weak. So we visualized the circle of the EU stars to move clockwise with such speed that a golden ring was formed, a symbol of unity. Finally the golden ring was extended into a sphere to embrace Europe and strengthen and demonstrate its integrity.

Creative rituals

The triangle described above is crucially important in performing geomantic rituals—it includes:

- the power of imagination,
- the clarity of visualization, plus
- the underlying emotional energy.

This triangle represents the basis of what we presented above as "creative rituals." We now need to add a fourth element, the physical component:

- lighting a candle,
- bowing in reverence, and
- supporting the given visualizations through body movements and other actions.

The physical component or structure may be of particular importance when we work as a group. Actions such as moving in the same rhythm, speaking the purpose of the given ritual, and singing will strengthen the ritual work.

Do not underestimate the artistic component that can strengthen and support creative rituals. Performance is not the end goal. But please remember that the world of elemental beings and environmental spirits loves "multimedia performances." Just look at the rituals performed by aborigines of different continents. They use a multitude of sounds, plenty of colors, and constantly repeat rhythmical movements.

I do not suggest the abundance of form on the physical level should be taken as an ideal model. The mechanistic multimedia market has made this model corrupt. However, imagination is the key to a new ritualistic richness. Elemental beings and other spirits of the Earth Cosmos are moving, as we are, into a new phase of evolution. This new phase is closely associated with consciousness and its ability to create through imagination. Beautifully coloring your face in your imagination might be of more value to the world of nature than if you do it physically.

Exercise 1
To purify a place of mental and emotional rubbish, a group disperses throughout that place. Each person imagines a ball of light and rolls it across the area. Like rolling a snowball, imagine that all the rubbish sticks to the ball, which becomes bigger and bigger. Next the group pushes all of the balls together to a previously chosen location, then stands around that location. It visualizes a violet color, the color of transmutation, to purify the energy caught in the mental and emotional rubbish and to help it return to the state of pure light.

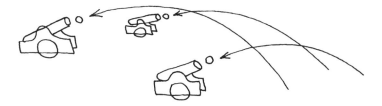

Example

To work with the traumas imprinted into the city organism of Prague during the siege by the Prussian army in the eighteenth century, we went as a group to Smíhow, the hill from where the army's cannons shot mercilessly upon the city below. Each member of the group imagined standing beside a gun. We imagined that the cannonballs that had been directed upon the city, together with the pain they caused, were returned to enter the mouths of the cannons, to find peace.

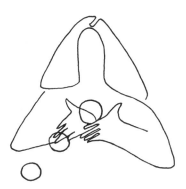

Exercise 2

If you are working with a place that has gone through much distress, use the exercise of tears of compassion (best used as a group). Position your hands as a channel in front of your heart. Imagine a tear in the form of a crystal ball emerging out of your heart center. Your hands direct the crystal ball to where it is needed, to a close or very distant location. When the tear touches the place, its content disperses. Briefly follow the distribution of its qualities to make sure that the place has absorbed them.

Magic ball

It is not by chance that all of the three examples described above are connected to the secret power of the ball. The ball is a symbol that fascinates. There are millions of football (soccer) fans that passionately focus their attention on the black and white sphere rolling over a playground. At the same time there are other millions of people who venerate a Holy Virgin icon standing on a ball. Even the Son that she is holding in her lap often holds a ball in his tiny hands. Such different scenes are linked to one and the same principle, to the "sphere of wholeness"!

Our geomantic research has found that each holon tends to become a ball. Its space cannot be flat or like a square. Its energies always display the tendency of rounding into a spherical form. Over the past years I even observed that the Earth Soul itself is furthering its self-healing process by using the ball principle. We mentioned the Islands of Light in an earlier chapter. They always appear in the form of a perfect ball, containing the vision of the Earth as a paradise.

Based on such observations I began to use the power of the ball in the course of geomantic and Earth healing work. But no physical balls are needed! The power of the ball can even intensify if used through the means of imagination. Using a ball calls and brings forth the wholeness of the universe into action.

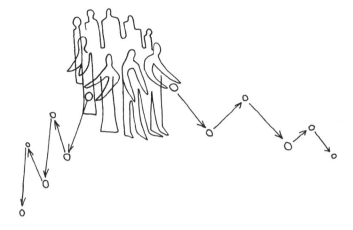

Example 1
While working as a group in Bloomington Park, Minneapolis, USA, a highly evolved elemental being suggested the following ritual to us to help distribute its qualities. We stood in a circle around the being's focus, with our backs turned to it. From the elemental being each person imagined receiving, through his or her back, a ball filled with the given qualities. Then a gesture of throwing the ball was performed. Through our imagination we followed each ball as it bounced forward in the landscape in front of us. We imagined that each time the ball touched the ground, information was distributed.

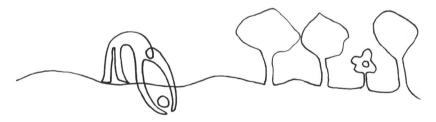

Example 2
To support the original quality of a place, imagine moving your hands underground to find a ball containing those original qualities. Lift that ball to the surface of the place, open it like an egg, and let the inherent qualities flow out over the place. Repeat the exercise few times, which is most effective when performed by a group.

Sound, color, and movement

Imaginations become even more creative if they are linked to a more physical form or body, not just a consciousness body as when we create visualizations. Imaginations are connected to a physical form when we make an effort to manifest them in our daily reality through our actions. Sound, color, and movement represent alternative kinds of form for imaginations—a much more subtle, yet manifested form.

Creative rituals based upon visualization are usually directed by mental concepts that state their precise purpose. Sound, color, and movement are tools that operate on a level beyond conscious control, at a level that is basically intuitive. Therein resides their creative power. Within the framework of the geomantic practice developed with my daughters Ana and Ajra since 1992, we have used singing (toning) in groups in geomantic work. The basis of group toning is the acupressure concept of applying pressure upon a given point. Toning at a particular spot works in the same way as applying the pressure of a finger upon an acupuncture point.

Different types of singing can be used as described in my book *Healing the Heart of the Earth*—but there is a basic form to it. The group stands in concentric circles gathered around a chosen spot, holding hands to allow synergy to enfold. After a short attunement, and possibly after stating the purpose of the work, singing begins, following the intuitive impulses of each person. We use vowels as a common singing basis. Each participant seeks to sing her or his role within the group toning, while listening to others. Singing develops as a process of intuitive and emotional interaction between the group and the multidimensional environment.

As each phenomena of the multidimensional world has its own sound vibration, it has also a characteristic color quality, as well as its own movement code. Working through sound, color, and movement (dance) it is possible to enter into an interaction with all of the different aspects of a place or landscape. These are wonderful, creative tools for being creative within invisible worlds, especially if healing, tuning, or balancing a landscape or environment is needed.

Colors can be used as part of creative rituals and applied through visualization. They can also be applied physically, providing a more permanent result. But be aware that colors can be creative at different levels. If one uses a color system based upon its symbolic meaning as a tool for geomantic work, the effects will be related to the spiritual level. The same colors may perform different roles if used upon the emotional plane. Their effect can be different yet again if they are applied to move energies, for example in the case of color system presented in my book *Healing the Heart of the Earth.*

We usually use the ancient form of circular dances if movement is chosen as a group working tool. But instead of re-creating traditional dance patterns, it is possible to create a pattern of movement that corresponds to the characteristic vibration of a given place and its actual situation. For example, if a place is out of balance it is possible to design a pattern of movement to re-establish its equilibrium.

A particular dance pattern can be designed as a key where the essence of the given place or landscape is coded. When such a key is repeatedly impressed upon the Earth surface through the steps of the dancing group, the possible blockages of the place are unlocked, and its natural beauty and harmony tend to manifest.

For more details about working through sound, color, and movement, please see *Healing the Heart of the Earth.*

Exercise 1
This drawing shows how a group is positioned while performing geomantic work through toning.

Exercise 2
This exercise is designed to purify a place through color imagi-
nation, using violet as the color of transmutation and white as
the color of perfection. The first step is to collect what needs to
be purified. Imagine that from the core of the Earth a wealth
of violet color is streaming to the surface and filling the whole
space of the environment. Ask that all distorted or destructive
vibrations within the place be attached to the violet color for
transmutation. The second step is to initiate the transmutation
process, imagining that the violet color is turning bit by bit into
bright white, until the whole place vibrates pure white. Give
thanks.

Silent co-creators

Creative rituals can be more effective if beings of other dimensions of existence are invited to collaborate. The invitation itself can be included as a part of the ritual. But I do not suggest any kind of formality. My experience has shown that the group spirit of a given animal species is willing to engage fully to help make an exercise or ritual succeed if it can relate to the purpose of the work. The same can be said for the spirits of ancestors/descendants or for elemental beings. They are perfect invisible helpers if the relationship between their role in the ritual and its purpose is clear.

For example, consider the animal soul protectors of places and countries. It is generally known that different countries refer to different animal species as their spiritual guides and protectors. They usually appear formally in connection with their coat of arms. Austria, for example, relates to a double-headed eagle, and the Czech Republic to a double-tailed lion. To include them as part of a ritual means to invite the given animal's soul essence to collaborate in that ritual. As a consequence, a specific energy or quality can manifest to take part in the work with the corresponding country or place.

If help from the side of ancestors/descendants is requested and granted, it is important not to become dependent on their guidance.

Any dependence of this kind can endanger the purpose of our spiritual path, which is intended to lead toward individual responsibility. Be careful to retain personal autonomy while accepting the help from invisible counselors.

New possibilities for collaboration with elemental beings and environmental spirits are available as different groups of these beings undergo their own transformations and as they become capable of co-creating with human beings. (Remember our statements about changes in the elemental world included in Chapter 3.5.) The dimensions of this possibility still need to be explored.

Example 1
After working on the previously mentioned Robins Wood Hill near Gloucester, England, we decided as a group to distribute its precious energies throughout the landscape by repeating the following ritual. Each participant performs a movement with her or his hands, taking a seed from the Hill permeated with its qualities. Then the hands are opened, an imaginary bird flies down, takes the seed, and carries it out to a certain point in the surrounding landscape. We were amazed at how many different kinds of birds came to help.

Example 2
The avenue called The Mall in Central Park, New York City, is associated with a path of ancestors. As a group, each one of us imagined having a golden bowl in her or his hands. We asked the ancestors to guide each person to places where they know emotional rubbish is hidden. (They can perceive at levels where our perception is weak.) We gathered the rubbish in bowls and brought it to a place where we worked on its transmutation, as described in the example above.

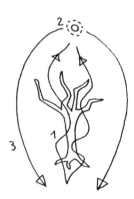

Example 3
A beautiful old apple tree has to be cut down. We gather as a group around the tree and ask the spirit of the tree to leave its home consciously, so that no trace of resentment will remain. As a group we create a strong field of love and appreciation around the tree. The spirit withdraws its presence from the root and trunk, and finally out of the tree crown (1). It ascends to the point of its spiritual focus and identifies with it (2). From there it descends along the surface of the aura that we have created down into the Earth, without touching the tree (3).

Exercise
"The bunny exercise" is helpful for distributing the special qualities of a place throughout the larger countryside, or even the Earth as a whole. Shape the given quality into an egg and call the Easter rabbit to come. Give the rabbit the egg and immediately direct it to run to the place that you have chosen, to leave the egg there as a seed for the given quality to evolve. Repeat a few times with different places that need that quality.

Cosmograms, zoograms

When imaginative messages are translated into graphic form, we speak of "cosmograms." Ancient cultures knew them as pictograms, hieroglyphs, or hermetic symbols. They represent visual signs in which a multidimensional message is coded. Cosmograms carrying multidimensional content are not conveying a logical message like modern signs created for different practical or symbolic purposes. Cosmograms are carrying a message coded on different levels simultaneously. On one side they can be perceived as energetic patterns; from another perspective as a codification of a cosmic archetype; on yet another level as visual signs.

As a consequence, cosmograms can serve as means of communication for contacting consciousness on different levels of existence.

- They can be used as a medium to contact spiritual or elemental beings that are not able to perceive messages in their physical form.

- They can be implemented to move energies and create communication bridges on the invisible levels.

- They are equally useful for conveying messages to the logical mind, which perceives exclusively on the physical level.

- They can become carriers of soul presence—transmitters of different spiritual qualities.

To be able to serve as pluridimensional signs, cosmograms should be created as a synthesis of logical and intuitive creative processes. Working on the aesthetic level is supplemented with artistic inspiration that comes into being through a heart-to-heart communication with the place for which the given cosmogram is being created.

Cosmograms have a peculiarity that distinguishes them from all other kinds of symbols. They must be created in such a way that they are not just objective forms, but are imbued with their own quality of energy and their own consciousness. On one side they address the viewer on a personal level; on the other they are capable of relatively autonomous activity within a given environment. They work on the basis of mutual exchange between partners involved in communication. They do not perform the mere function of transmitting information as do ordinary symbols.

When the qualities and energies of certain animal species are involved in creating a cosmogram, the expression "zoogram" can be used. In a zoogram an animal form does not just represent a figure used to create the aesthetic form of a sign. The soul quality of the given animal species is invited to actively co-create the message, which is an integral part of "the silent activity" of the cosmogram.

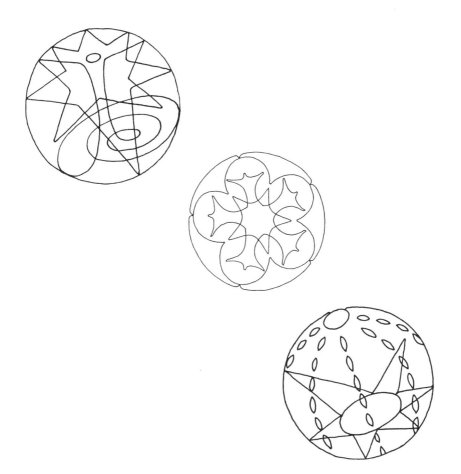

Example 1

This example shows three cosmograms created in 2006 by the author for the central axes of the territory of the county hospital of Klagenfurt, Austria. From left to right they relate to the root chakra, the heart chakra, and the crown chakra of the territory. Together with seven other cosmograms, some of them created by other artists from the Austrian geomancy group, carved in marble, they now stand on acupuncture points of the hospital's landscape.

Example 2
This example shows four cosmograms created in 2006 by the author for the lithopuncture project completed on both sides of the borders between Hungary, Slovenia, and Croatia. In a project financed by the European Union as an INTERREG cross-border project, ten other artists from the Slovenian geomancy group collaborated and carved their cosmograms in stone.

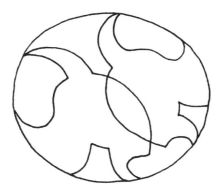

Example 3
This example shows a zoogram created by the author for protection against electromagnetic waves transmitted by such devices as power lines, telephones, and computers. The group soul of goats revealed itself as capable of performing such a role, related to a special kind of intelligence that goats embody.

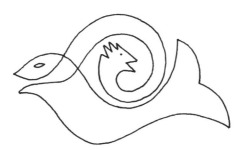

Example 4
This example shows a zoogram created in 2007 to strengthen the relationship of Venice, represented as a fish (Venice is built upon water and shows the form of a fish), and the place of Scuola Grande San Giovanni, symbolized by a spiraling dragon.

Holographic exercises

If the principle of creating cosmograms is translated into movement, we speak of holographic movements. "Holographic" means that such movements are embodying a holistic message that is capable of entering into resonance with different worlds, qualities, or places. Holographic movements are created to perform a specific service within the energy fields of those worlds, qualities, or energy fields. Ancient cultures understood and used holographic exercises in their praying gestures, trance postures, and repetitive dance movements.

A complete set of holographic exercises that I learned in different places around the world can be found in my book *Earth Changes, Human Destiny*. In these exercises body movements or postures are combined with imaginations.

Exercise 1
This exercise is designed to connect Earth and Heaven. I was shown this holographic exercise by the spirit of Crete, Greece.

1. *Squat (with your knees bent) to represent yourself as a symbol of the cosmos coming closer to the Earth.*
2. *Raise your hands so that your palms are level with your throat as a symbol of the Earth moving closer to the cosmos.*
3. *Remain in this position for awhile and imagine that your hands and knees are holding a pillar of white light which reaches deep into the Earth and high up toward the cosmos.*

Exercise 2
This exercise is intended to support the identity of Israel/Palestine. I was taught the exercise by the consciousness of the Dead Sea landscape.

1. *Lie down on your belly. Your back represents the desert landscape extending from the Red Sea to the Dead Sea depression.*
2. *Now position your left hand across your back to touch your right hip. With this movement the torso turns forward, representing Jerusalem, the heart center of the country. It is also the turning point that reveals the front side of the body.*
3. *Be aware of your throat center opened to the space around you, and turn your head accordingly. This movement represents the Sea of Galilee as the organ of communication with the larger world.*

Lithopuncture, xylopuncture, geopuncture

Lithopuncture is a method of Earth acupuncture that I developed in the early 1980s. Creating a lithopuncture project involves exploring a place or landscape through the means of geomancy, deciding which points need to be treated, and then positioning stone pillars with carved cosmogrames. The Greek word "lithos" means "stone," and "punctura" is a Latin word meaning "a stitch."

Ancient cultures used similar methods by positioning stones or stone circles on certain points in the landscape, a method that can be compared with acupressure. The stone is positioned so it presses properly at a sensitive point on the landscape. In this way a constant impulse is being transmitted to the organism of the place. It may be an impulse of balancing, acceleration, or honoring its power and intelligence.

The same principles apply to lithopuncture. But I have gained a new insight that corresponds to this era in which consciousness plays a guiding role. The direction in which the positioned stone works, be it on energetic or soul level, is defined or directed by the cosmogram carved in its surface. So the role of the stone within the whole composition of lithopuncture stones and within the whole environment is clearly communicated to the different levels of consciousness that a cosmogram can embrace.

A lithopuncture project is usually conceived as a composition of a number of stone pillars with cosmograms. If the placement of stones cannot be undertaken in a location, the cosmogram can be cast in bronze and laid into the pavement. Also, wooden poles can be used for Earth acupuncture. In this case the rhythm of driving the poles into the ground is the main impulse-giving tool. I speak of xylopuncture ("xylos"—Greek for "wood") when a cosmograme is being driven into the ground through wooden poles.

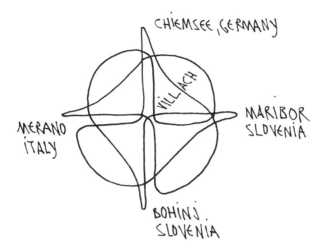

Example 1

This example shows a composition of five lithopuncture stones called "Star of the Alps," created in 1997 by the author and his wife and commissioned by the town council of Villach, Austria. Stones with cosmogrames are positioned in Germany, Italy, Slovenia, and Austria along two ley-lines that cross each other close to Villach. The purpose of the work is to strengthen the integrity of the region of the Alps that is weakened by rapid urbanization.

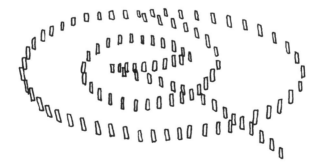

Example 2

A work of xylopuncture that the author created in 2004 in front of the Museum of Modern Art in Ljubljana, Slovenia. The cosmogram relates to the role of Ljubljana within the greater Europe holon.

5.2 Geomancy as a language to communicate with the Earth

Considering the different practical aspects of geomantic research, first we need to emphasize the urgent need for us, as individuals and as a civilization, to know and understand our home planet in a holistic way. As we confront and try to prevent far-reaching ecological changes and possible catastrophes, our first step is to open our minds and hearts to the Earth and all her potentials and dimensions. There is no doubt that it is possible to find optimum solutions in cooperation with the planet's consciousness and by activating our soul link with the Earth.

However, current geographical knowledge and material values, together with an exclusively mental approach to the Earth and its evolutions, does not provide an adequate framework for developing a new kind of relationship to the Earth. The project of developing a multidimensional kind of geography, which we call geomancy, is a serious attempt to open new paths of communication with our planet to secure our common harmonious future.

We can expect that rational minds will not be comfortable with or receptive to the pluridimensional concept that is the foundation for a modern geomancy. This work may be labeled and rejected as "esoteric" or even "New Age." Never mind:

- Rejection is common to situations when new insights and approaches begin to open.

- Rejection is a creative challenge through which geomantic knowledge can be developed in a more grounded and communicative way.

- Be patient—rational science is even now developing concepts approaching a pluridimensional space of reality that can be acceptable to open, logical thinking.

The task that connects all, lovers of the Earth Cosmos, is two-fold:

- To develop the language and practice of geomancy so that its knowledge and practical projects can be accepted within public awareness and by the consciousness of modern-minded people who are basically open to change.

- To further our projects of communication with the Earth as a whole and all its different dimensions and beings.

Example
Geopuncture circles project
Compositions of stones with cosmograms called "geopuncture circles"
are designed to enable communication of the human world with the
Earth Soul concerning the process of ongoing planetary changes and our
common future. They are composed of a large number of lithopuncture
stones with cosmograms carved or designed by groups of people from
different countries. The name "geopuncture circles" conveys the premise that the Earth as a whole is touched and affected by acupuncture
projects, not single, individual places.

Each project is composed around a specific theme. The geopuncture
circle "Solar Plexus of Europe" was built in Zagreb, Croatia, in 2005.
It is composed of 61 granite blocks with cosmograms cast in bronze. Its
theme is related to places, landscapes and qualities that are of critical
importance for realigning the center of Europe that pulsates between
Frankfurt, Prague, Zagreb, Milan, and Bern. The project constructed
in Tamera, Portugal in 2005-06 consists of 58 stones. Its theme is the
emerging society of peace.

5.3 Holistic ecology

The worldwide ecological movement has accomplished a great deal to prevent further destruction of the natural environment. Unfortunately some aspects of living and breathing ecosystems do not receive the attention and care that they deserve. The importance of these aspects of ecosystems does not refer to the physical level of existence, but to the subtle levels that are not recognized by natural sciences. However, it is exactly these levels that geomancy addresses.

Complementing scientific ecology with geomancy means discovering new objectives and understanding why certain places and aspects of natural and urban environments must be protected to secure a sustainable interrelationship of nature, landscape, and human culture. It means acknowledging and understanding centers of elemental/environmental beings responsible for the balanced evolution of a given landscape, and places through which the Earth Soul is touching a given landscape and ecosystem to imbue it with the necessary life force and energy.

Actually the ecological movement is much more pluralistic than may be reflected by public opinion. There already are different layers of ecological interest, research, study, and practice that share values and concerns with holistic ecology:

- The *personal ecology movement* includes a multitude of individuals worldwide who are advocating for changes in our attitudes toward the living environment and in our habits regarding water, energy, waste, land use, urban sprawl, agriculture, forestry, and so forth.

- *Scientific ecology* has been given increasing public and political support. Research, education, legislative programs, and funding are being invested—albeit not enough—to protect the biosphere of landscapes, seas, and the atmosphere.

- *Deep ecology and ecopsychology authors* have introduced to ecology the psychological, psychic, philosophical, and spiritual dimensions of the Earth, nature, and the environment. A deeper understanding is being opened regarding the complexity and interrelationships of humans, plant and animal kingdoms, sacred nature, and the Earth.

- *Holistic ecology* currently is scarcely recognized in the awareness of the public. Its task is to introduce a pluridimensional view of life, the planet, and the landscape to our civilization and to the practice of ecology. The landscape phenomena that modern holistic geomancy is exploring must be integrated into society and ecology—these phenomena include etheric organs, the Earth Soul presence, environmental spirits, landscape temple structures, and other levels of the Earth Cosmos needed to sustain and enable life on Earth to flourish.

Example
A biodynamic farmer from Mellstorf, Switzerland, demanded geomantic research conducted by the author before and after a gas pipeline was installed across his land. The pipeline company approved and financed it. It was discovered that the pressure in the pipelines is causing the land to loose its original quality of grounding. The place has been grounded anew through lithopuncture and the planting of corresponding trees.

5.4 Geomancy as environmental healing

A specific area of creativity in the landscape and in cities that was developed by the modern geomancy movement is the domain of environmental healing. In general, the approach of traditional ecology is often defensive and protective. Restoration ecology—applied to damaged or deteriorated ecosystems—has advanced greatly as a complementary approach. But there seem to be innumerable situations where nothing can be done to address or redress environmental degradation and conditions that seriously and adversely compromise, impact, or threaten the health, integrity and well-being—or even survival—of the landscape and the diverse populations of beings that depend upon it. For example, it is generally not possible to remove or relocate a motorway because its location has severed an important energy flow in the landscape. It is generally not possible to demolish and restore an entire neighborhood of a city that has been constructed on a sacred place of nature.

This is an area where geomancy and its methods of environmental healing can be of great help and service. Working with dimensions of reality that transcend the level of material manifestation, and using the geomantic approaches and tools described above, it is possible to release and restore healing impulses in many different situations, for example:

- when vital-energy centers or flows of vital powers have been blocked or weakened by urban development, industrial expansion, mining, and other forms of development or human manipulation of the environment;

- when the balance between the feminine and masculine powers in the landscape has been distorted, as in the suppression of natural flows of water or the constructing of artificial lakes and other water bodies;

- when the vital powers of a place have been manipulated through the misuse of power for ideological or spiritual purposes;

- when nature sanctuaries or other focuses of elemental beings and environmental spirits have been drastically changed, and these beings become alienated from the natural order and intelligence of that area; and

- when landscapes become victims of war, conflict, and other atrocities.

The list could be much longer. Within the context of the present book it is possible only to make short statements on how geomantic knowledge and practice can become useful within modern society and within the personal lives of individuals. For practical examples related to environmental healing, see *Healing the Heart of the Earth*.

5.5 Geomancy as a path of self-knowledge

It is not by chance that our evolution has incarnated upon the Earth. But incarnating upon the Earth looses its sense, its reason for being, if the earthly environment is used only for any number of self-centered purposes. Being incarnated upon the Earth means that we human beings are challenged with the joyful task of becoming co-creators with what I call the Earth Cosmos. It is simply not possible to fully develop as human beings if we neglect our bonds that connect us with the Earth Soul and sister evolutions.

The privilege and challenge that the Earth offers us is the opportunity to experience the results and consequences of our visions, decisions, and actions as psychological or even bodily reactions. There is an immense potential of learning and teaching to be gained through the direct experience offered through the Earth's space of reality. On the other hand, the creative potential that we human beings can offer to the worlds of the Earth is our virtually limitless and at times even crazy capability to invent and create something new and unexpected.

The possibilities for a co-creative relationship, a true partnership with the Earth Cosmos, are present, before us, but how can they become a reality if we know the Earth only superficially, relating only to the rational framework of traditional geography and our material culture?

Participating in the development of a new geomancy can have an even greater impact upon the personal spiritual path of a person if we consider the Earth Cosmos as mirroring our individual microcosm. As children of the Earth Soul we inherit all her dimensions and qualities, but in a state of potentiality. By knowing and understanding the dimensions and qualities of the multidimensional body of Gea, through experiencing them within places and landscapes, we develop the capability and the blessing to recognize the same powers and qualities within our personal holon—and to awaken them to their full blossoming. In this sense, the Earth Cosmos can be considered as a place of initiation. Sacred Geography is mapping the Earth in the way to help individuals to find their own path of initiation into the secrets of creation, peace, love, balance, harmony, and service.

5.6 Geomantic knowledge in architecture, urban planning, and environmental design

As we examine the contents of Sacred Geography it becomes obvious that the approach of geomantic knowledge has direct relevance to such endeavors as architecture, landscape architecture, and urban, land use and environmental planning. These and other areas of human creativity and related professional disciplines directly affect the geomantic systems of the Earth surface. Unfortunately geomantic knowledge is not yet taught in our colleges, universities, and other institutions of learning.

Concerning architecture, urban and land use planning, environmental design, and other related fields, there are several points related to Sacred Geography that need to be considered. The land or area to be developed should be investigated to identify:

- whether there are geomantic phenomena that should be protected from construction and development, and perhaps preserved in areas such as parks or bioreserves; and

- whether there are places within the given landscape that radiate in a way that is not suitable for human beings. These places need not be considered "negative," but at the same time they should not be utilized as places for human habitation or related activities—or they should be properly adjusted to the proposed new function through geomantic methods.

In the case of architectural planning and design, geomantic properties are important not only for the proper placement and alignment of a building, but also for attuning the planned architecture with the energies and qualities of the given place. Further, geomantic exploration of the surrounding area might reveal powers and properties that can be integrated into the architectural design.

Through geomantic knowledge, the architect (using the term in both a professional and more general sense) can consciously introduce new powers and qualities into the given ambience or environment, using corresponding proportions, forms, symbolic figures, colors, and so forth. Instead of being an act of destruction to the natural environment, building can become a co-creative act through which an architectural work is capable of introducing new qualities to a project or place. Here are some geomantic methods that can be useful in the design work:

- using the Yin-Yang polarization of elements to play a role in the design;
- creating forms that stimulate the flow of etheric powers;
- incorporating cosmograms into the forms of a building or exterior/interior design;
- introducing the effects of resonance.

A similar geomantic approach can be used in designing or crafting smaller objects. For example, the material used in designing an object can offer its etheric vibrations and its consciousness as a possible field of co-creation with the sacred powers of the Earth Soul. It depends on the sensibility and intuition of the designer to what extent the subtle qualities or energies of the material can be integrated into the work.

5.7 Developing profound tourism

Since times immemorial people have walked pilgrimage paths to visit sacred places of the Earth Cosmos. Nowadays we are witnesses of another kind of pilgrimage—tourism. Millions of people are on the move to visit the places and landscapes of their desire.

To prevent tourism from becoming a major component of environmental destruction, it is possible to combine it with the ancient concept of pilgrimage. It is perfectly appropriate to visit foreign countries and cities to enjoy the variability of life and culture. We return home loaded with gifts of foreign countries. But what have we given the countries and people that we have visited beyond some undetermined economic benefit? To prevent the potential destructive effects of tourism and to discover a more sensible way to travel and vacation, the cycle of receiving and giving must be balanced.

The knowledge of geomancy can provide travelers with the tools to deepen their contact with the land or culture they visit, and to create an exchange of energy between the visitor and the visited place. Instead of the superficial information often provided by tourist guides, the knowledge of geomancy can help one experience places or aspects of the environment that may be otherwise hidden to the curiosity of the rational mentality.

The pilgrimage dimension of travel and tourist routes emerges when people can perceive the places they visit as mirroring certain aspects of their own true nature, thus helping them on the path of their own spiritual development. These places and landscapes in turn receive the kind of attention that supports their true identity and function and helps them fulfil their respective role in life within the Earth Cosmos. The cycle of communion, of communication and exchange, evolves and deepens as we co-create a multidimensional world of mutual respect, love, and cooperation.

Code of ethics underlying the work with the living universe

Understanding that a code of ethics is based upon the personal freedom to choose, decide, and act accordingly, I believe that it is important to propose a code of ethics and behavior that is not intended to be an obligatory guideline. Rather, it is a manifesto voiced in the presence of the Earth Soul and its living conditions for our mutual communication and emerging co-operation, proposed in the name of a new art of geomancy and its practitioners.

The seven principles described below are derived from the drawing on the following page of a vision of a newly developing civilization of peace. The inner development of each individual is of decisive importance for the loving and co-creative relationship of human civilization towards the Earth Cosmos to become manifest.

Let us work on renewing our sensibility.
The exclusive dependence upon our five senses for perception has resulted in the narrowing and flattening of the sensitivity of the modern human to one single level of perception. We must work personally on renewing the natural quality of human perception which in its essence is pluridimensional.

The iron logics of the rational consciousness has to be integrated.
Human rationality is rapidly progressing toward an exclusive control over our personal lives and over the worlds surrounding us. Our response must be to develop its counterpart, the intuitive way of thinking, and yet honor the qualities of the logical mind and integrate them into the universal language through which different levels and dimensions of life can communicate freely.

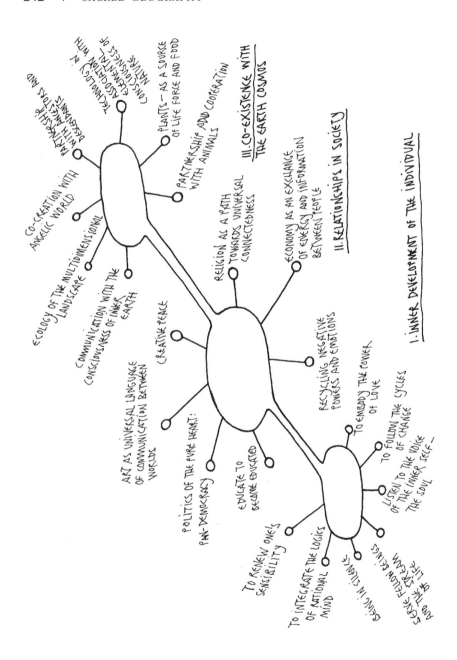

Blueprint of a new civilization of peace. A drawing done by the author for the exhibition 2000+23, Museum of Modern Art, Ljubljana, 2006.

Be at peace.
We should cultivate and hold an inner peace in this hectic, rapidly changing world. Holding peace within the dimensions of our individual lives means that we create the possibility for peace in the larger world.

Serve the flow of life.
A large host of beings, visible and invisible, are helping each one of us at any moment to fulfil our life's purpose—even to exist. To complete the cycle, each of us should find ways to help other beings of life and support them on their paths, regardless of the level of existence at which they are pulsating.

Listen to the voice of your soul.
At the soul level human beings are one with all other beings and dimensions of the living universe. Listen to the silent voice of your own soul, to its subtle forms of expression, and you will be in tune with the Earth Soul, the essence of each living being, and the universal self that human cultures call God or Goddess.

Honor the cycles of change.
We are living within a universe that is evolving toward perfection. Accept the imperfect and faulty conditions of life within and around you. Seek possibilities to enrich life with more beauty and perfection.

Embody the power and gentleness of love.
If you find yourself in a world denying your desire for love and beauty, see it as a challenge to love more deeply. Love gives freedom to each of us, all members of the universe, to be who we truly are. Love enables each one of us to make others happy, to support their creative intent, and to make the universe flow.

Marko Pogačnik was born in 1944 in Kranj, Slovenia. He graduated in 1967 as a sculptor from the Academy of Fine Arts in Ljubljana. He lives with his family in Šempas, Slovenia.

From 1965 to 1971 he worked as a member of the OHO group in the fields of conceptual and landscape art. Exhibitions included the Information Show in 1970 at the Museum of Modern Art in New York, USA; Aktionsraum, in Munich, Germany, in 1970; and the Global Conceptualism Show 1950-80, at the Queens Museum of Art, New York, USA, 1999.

In 1971 he founded a rural and artistic community with his family and friends, the "Šempas Family," at Šempas, Slovenia. This community existed until 1978. Exhibitions included Trigon 1977 in Graz, Austria, and the Venice Biennalle of 1978 in Venice, Italy.

Since 1979 he has been engaged in geomantic and Earth healing work. In the mid-1980s he began to develop a method of Earth healing similar to acupuncture, using stone pillars with carved cosmograms, positioned on acupuncture points in a landscape. He calls this Earth healing work "lithopuncture."

Marko's lithopuncture works include:

❖ Lithopuncture of two castle parks in Germany, Türnich (1986-89) and Cappenberg (1988-92).

❖ Lithopuncture of the territory on both sides of the border between North Ireland and the Republic of Ireland, Orchard Gallery, Derry (1991-92).

❖ Lithopuncture of the urban environments of Villach (1995), Klagenfurt, (1998), Bad Radkersburg (2001), Austria; Nova Gorica, Slovenia (2001-02); Quito, Ecuador (2003); St.Veit, Austria (2004); Zagreb, Croatia (2004); Prague, Czech Republic (2005-06); Bad Pyrmont, Germany (2006).

❖ "Alpenstern," a trans-Alps lithopuncture project with lithopuncture stones in Italy (Merano), Austria (Villach), Slovenia (Maribor) and Germany (Chiemsee) (1997).

❖ Lithopuncture of Circuito das Aguas, Minas Gerais, Brazil (1998). Seeland lithopuncture network, Switzerland (1998-2002).

❖ Aachen lithopuncture network, Ludwig Forum Aachen, (1999).

❖ Lithopuncture project on both sides of the border between Austria and Slovenia in Carinthia (1999-2002).

❖ In the years 2005-2007 Marko has participated in the collective creation of geopuncture stone circles in Zagreb, Tamera (Portugal), and Prague.

Marko's books in English:
Nature Spirits and Elemental Beings (1996)
Healing the Heart of the Earth (1998)
Christ Power and the Earth Goddess (1999)
Earth Changes, Human Destiny (2000)
The Daughter of Gaia (2001)
Turned Upside Down (2004)
How Wide the Heart (together with Ana Pogačnik, 2006)
Touching the Breath of Gaia (2007)

In 1991 Marko Pogačnik designed the official coat of arms and the flag of the newly constituted Republic of Slovenia.

In addition to his writing and lithopuncture projects, Marko leads workshops in environmental healing throughout the world. Together with his daughters Ana and Ajra he teaches long-term education courses on geomancy and personal development in Sweden, Germany, Italy, Austria, Slovenia, Switzerland, and the United States. He is president of the Hagia Chora School for Geomancy in Germany and is a faculty member of the Omega Institute in the USA.

Together with his daughter Ana and other collaborators, in 1997 he created LifeWeb, a worldwide Network for Geomancy and Transformation.
To contact the North American group, see www.lifenethome.org
To contact the Great Britain group, see www.earthenergynetwork.co.uk

An ongoing program in geomancy and personal development in North America is organized by SteinerBooks, Great Barrington, Massachusetts (the first two-year course was held 2006-2007).
For further information, see www.steinerbooks.org and www.lifenethome.org.

Internet home page: http://www.pogacnikmarko.com
Address: Marko Pogačnik, Šempas 160, Si-5261 Šempas, Slovenia